Unleash Your Dreams
Going Beyond Goal Setting

Stephen Oliver

www.stephenoliverblog.com

Copyright © 2013 by Stephen Oliver

First Published 2013 by Stephen Oliver

ISBN: 978-0-9927441-0-6 (Kindle eBook)

ISBN: 978-0-9927441-1-3 (Paperback)

Excellent book! In-depth and packed with insights!

Dr Joe Vitale, author "The Attractor Factor"

Many roads lead to Success.

Buy this book to find the road which suits you. The author is proficient in NLP and honors the fact that individuals tick differently. Thus, he offers each type of individual learning tools matching particular needs and capabilities. Amusing with fine British humor and generously sprinkled with inspiring quotes, the work is a compilation of useful techniques always with one goal in mind: Success!

René Vögtli, Reiki Master Teacher,
author "Reiki, der Weltverbesserer",
co-founder RIO Reiki International Organisation

I have had the privilege of reading Stephen's book, and I was blown away by the simplicity of such a potentially complex subject. Stephen has presented the facts in a way anyone could understand, giving real life examples and creating analogies that are both possible and coherent.

This book is a must read for anyone wanting to find a way to understand themselves, their goals and how to reach what they truly desire.

Mandy Allen, www.mandyallen.com

Disclaimer

All the material contained in this eBook is provided for educational and informational purposes only. No responsibility can be taken for any results or outcomes resulting from the use of this material.

All information should be carefully studied, independently researched, and clearly understood before taking any action based on the information or advice in this eBook. While every attempt has been made to provide information that is both accurate and effective, the Author and Publisher does not assume any responsibility for the accuracy, omissions, contrary interpretation of the subject matter herein, or use / misuse of this information.

Any perceived slights of specific persons, peoples, or organizations are unintentional.

In practical advice eBooks, like anything else in life, there are no guarantees of income made. Readers are cautioned to rely on their own judgment about their individual circumstances to act accordingly. The Author and Publisher assumes no responsibility or liability whatsoever on behalf of any Purchaser or Reader of these materials. The Purchaser or Reader of this publication assumes full responsibility for the use of these materials and information.

This eBook is not intended for use as a source of legal, business, accounting or financial advice. All readers are advised to seek services of competent professionals in legal, business, accounting and finance fields.

The information in this eBook is not intended to be a substitute for professional mental health advice. Diagnosis and treatment of a clinical condition can only be undertaken by a qualified mental health professional. Readers of this eBook should always seek the advice of a qualified health professional with any questions they have regarding their health or a medical condition. If you find the information and exercises in this eBook cause you distress, please stop immediately and consult a mental health professional.

Table of Contents

Table of Figures

Alphabetical List of Work Materials

Preface

> Begin at the beginning and go on till you come to the end; then stop.
>> Lewis Carroll, *"Alice's Adventures in Wonderland"*
>>> Said by the King to the White Rabbit

Why do <u>you</u> want to read this book?

Does any of these situations seem familiar to you?

- New Year's Resolutions

- "I'm definitely starting that diet tomorrow."

- "I really **must** …"

But somehow you never do …

We all know these situations; they occur with depressing regularity. The question is: Why?

After all, we know the benefits, or we wouldn't have made the resolutions and decisions in the first place. Something is getting in the way of success, but what could it be?

My experience, and quite possibly yours too, is one of the following:

- We either have no real idea where we want to go;

- We know where we want to go but we either have no idea how to start the journey;

- We have no idea how to complete it.

In other words, we need a methodology to follow to ensure that we know where we want to go, why we want to do it, how to start doing it, and how to know when we've got there. Furthermore, over time we develop a tendency to lose the commitment and enthusiasm we started with. We also need to learn how to handle this loss of motivation.

Although I will talk later about forgetting the "hows", we do need to know how to start, and how to maintain the energy.

A short personal history

I recently realised that I've been teaching for more than twenty-five years, and writing for even longer.

The writing began when I had to write a handbook. The company I worked for had developed asset-management software, and now needed user documentation for it. Although it was hard work, I thoroughly enjoyed it.

I started the teaching part of my career as a freelance lecturer for DEC (Digital Equipment Corporation, a now-defunct computer manufacturer). Later, after being one of the architects of a major system created by and for a large Swiss bank, I had to create the handbooks and training seminars for that software in both English and German. I taught the seminars in Switzerland, England and America, while a member of the programming team took over the Far East and Australia.

During the latter period, I learnt NLP (see the *Glossary* for an explanation of this and other terms), and also became a Reiki Master. I teach Reiki in England, Switzerland and Spain.

Some years ago, I decided that I should finally learn how to teach adults "properly," according to the accepted practices in Switzerland, where I lived for more than three decades, instead of the haphazard way I had been doing it up to then. The course was split into three modules and, although I learned a lot, as I completed each part, I realised that I'd already been doing the right thing instinctively.

As part of the coursework, I had to produce course plans and a concept for a course. This I based on Reiki courses, plus a course I had created some years earlier (*see Prelude to Dreaming: Introduction* on page 22).

Why __this__ book? And why now?

Now let's take a step to one side and look at why I resolved to write this book.

For my fiftieth birthday, I bought myself an Apple iPod, with 30 gigabytes capacity. I transferred all the music I owned and started downloading audiobooks from iTunes and Audible.com. By Easter of the following year, I was reaching the capacity of the iPod, and bought one with 80 gigabytes storage. I continued buying audiobooks. Nowadays, I use a 160 GB iPod Classic (for my music) and a 64GB iPod Touch (for audiobooks).

Among the various audiobooks I bought at the time, I found three authors whose work really impressed me: James Arthur Ray, Rhonda Byrne and Dr Joe Vitale. What they wrote (or rather said) hit me hard, since it confirmed that what I'd built into the course was based on real ideas.

In one of his books, Dr Vitale mentioned co-authoring an eBook with Jim Edwards called "*How to Write and Publish your own book ... in as little as 7 days*". I went to the Web site, liked what I saw, bought and downloaded it. As I read it, I was inspired to create an eBook of my own. The only question: "What should I write about?"

I talked to a friend who'd long spoken of writing a book on *Shojin Riori*, the Japanese cooking of Zen monasteries, but hadn't started doing anything about it. It turned out that he didn't think that his book would be a good idea to have on the Internet. I talked to my father, who had also mentioned writing a cookery book, but who also never got started with the project. He wasn't ready to get into it, either.

At this point, I realised that it was a case of "if you want it done, you must do it yourself." So I looked at the courses I had written or was working on, and this one sprang to mind, because it corresponded to what I'd been listening to during the previous couple of weeks.

I've reworked the course, writing in many of the parts that I'd normally tell my students directly, and leaving out parts that can only be carried out in groups, or are inappropriate in a book.

Here, then, is the book, which I hope you find useful. May your dreams be splendid, powerful and, above all, ***unleashed***!

Acknowledgements and Thanks

I'd like to thank the following people:

- Peter Wrycza, PhD, for reminding me on his course *Write On!* that I **could** write.

- The teachers of *The Living NLP Learning Community* during *Vision Bali 93* for teaching me the fundamentals of NLP: Jan Ardui, MA, Susan Grace Branch, MA, Michael Colgrass, Judith A. Delozier, MA, Anne K. Entus, PhD, Peter Wrycza, PhD.

- Dennis Jansen, PhD, for encouraging me to go down the path of personal development, for teaching me, and for being my friend.

- My friends Patricia Bollag, Mathias Woringer and Barbro Ericsson Villa, for helping me develop the original course.

- Kory Koontz, my coach on the *Miracles Coaching Course*, for helping me remove some of the blocks in my way, and Dr Joe Vitale, for developing the course.

- Tony Laidig and the members of the *Easy Book A Day* course of February 2013, for the information and help I got while preparing the book for publication.

- And finally, my Mother, our friends Lizzie Ahmedzai and Ann McMann, my Reiki Master Teacher René Vögtli, and Mandy Allen from John Thornhill's *One Month Mentor* program, for proofreading the book. Among other things, I wanted to see whether it made any sense to a lay person who knew nothing about self-development techniques.

Overview

I suggest you read the book through once to get a feel for what it's all about, then go back and do the exercises in order.

The book is divided into 5 parts:

Prelude to Dreaming

This is the theoretical part, preparing you for what's to come. It contains useful information we'll need later in the course, as it explains the background behind the course and includes the basic concepts behind of some of the exercises.

Creating the Dreams

This part is where you decide what dreams you want to make reality, and pass them through the steps necessary to make them compelling dreams for you to follow.

Living the Dreams

Here we pass on to methods and techniques to help you to carry your dreams through to the end. It helps you deal with blocks, lack of motivation, aligning yourself with your self, and it even shows a way to create new options and ideas.

Appendices

This contains a glossary with explanations of technical words used, a bibliography, including recommended eBooks, audio books and videos, and Internet links.

Work Materials

This is not an actual, physical section of the book. The exercises have been scattered throughout the book so you can do them as you work your way through the course.

The work materials are available individually for download as PDF and PDF Form files, as well as all together and in a zip file. These files can be found on the web page (http://unleash-your-dreams.com/downloads/). If you wish, you can download all the exercises as follows:

A single printable PDF file
(http://www.unleash-your-dreams.com/downloads/UYD -
Work Materials.pdf)

A single Zip file
(http://www.unleash-your-dreams.com/downloads/UYD - Work Materials.zip)

A collection of PDF Forms in a Zip File
(http://www.unleash-your-dreams.com/downloads/FUYD - Work Materials.zip).

PDF Forms are pages you can fill in directly on your computer. You have permission to print or copy them for your personal use.

Illustrations may also be found in a PDF file
(http://www.unleash-your-dreams.com/downloads/UYD - Illustrations.pdf), or in a Zip file (http://www.unleash-your-dreams.com/downloads/UYD - Illustrations.zip).

> *Quotes are shown like this.*
> Author

Stories that illustrate a point are written like this.

If you find phrases or terms you don't understand, you will find explanations in the *Glossary* on page 218, or the occasional endnote for non-NLP words.

PS. If you're American, accept an apology in advance for the spelling. I am British by birth, and thus spell my words that way.

Prelude to Dreaming

All men dream, but not equally. Those who dream by night in the dusty recesses of their minds wake in the day to find that it was vanity; but the dreamers of the day are dangerous men, for they may act their dream with open eyes, to make it possible.

T. E. Lawrence (Lawrence of Arabia),
"The Seven Pillars of Wisdom"

Introduction

At the beginning of the 80s, I was sent by my employers of the time to a goal-setting workshop. It was an interesting experience, but it didn't really "take". Something seemed to be missing.

In 1993, I attended an NLP Practitioner training course for a month in Bali, learning a great deal about using the techniques for personal development.

During the middle of the 90s, a group of friends and I (all of us NLP practitioners) started to look at the problems of goal-setting and similar courses we'd taken over the years, with a view to creating our own. I was designated as the main person because I was the only one with sufficient computer skills. Indeed, I did most of the actual work in designing and creating it, with some input from the others.

We determined several areas in which such courses had problems and deficiencies. Since then, these only seem to have become worse, with new issues joining the old.

Work / Career

Most goal-setting courses are generally orientated to work and career. Their primary concern is with success in the workplace, career and the daily processing of tasks. They're often connected to a particular system (FiloFax®, Time System®, etc.), and are sold in association with them.

At the end of the process, you'd have the following information:

1. What you want to achieve.

2. How much you want to achieve.

3. When you will achieve your goal.

Although these can be useful for some career and workplace goals, for goals and dreams in other areas of our lives, such as personal growth, etc., these methods are inadequate. We decided to research further into these other areas.

Stopping Short

Many goal-setting courses and books stop short of being complete because they give little information about what to do after setting the goals. They may provide general information about writing down a list of steps and going through them one at a time, but there is often nothing about reviews and changing direction if you find yourself off course. Also, little is said about dealing with obstacles along the way, and how to handle a loss of motivation.

"Fluffiness"

Despite the promises of the courses mentioned above, even career goals are often poorly formulated, since what we want to achieve is often expressed in a "fluffy" manner.

"Fluffy" means that the words sound as though they mean something, but have very different meanings for different people. It's a lot like eating cotton candy or candyfloss (this depends on whether you're American or English). It tastes nice, but when you start chewing on it, there's almost nothing there.

Terms such as "profitability", "profit margin", "progress", or even "rich" often have as many meanings as the number of people saying them. For example, Dr David Schwartz, speaking at a seminar in America, asked 100 top managers taking part to give a definition of "profitability". He received 98 entirely different and mutually incompatible answers (three of the managers came from the same company, so their descriptions were very similar).

Similarly, "rich" might mean having an extra discretionary income of $500 a month for one person, while for another it means owning assets totalling many millions.

There have to be better methods of defining these goals, especially for such areas as personal growth. This leads us to the next point.

Criteria are insufficient

The three criteria (what / how much / when) are inadequate for personal goals. Goals such as "improving the quality of my life", "bettering my knowledge of computers", "finding love", or even "having a million" aren't completely definable using such criteria. They're better measured using affective (emotional) rather than cognitive (rational) benchmarks.

By using criteria based on the senses (primarily seeing, hearing and feeling), you can better determine when you're approaching or achieving a goal.

Motivation

One of the greatest problems, especially in the area of personal growth, is that of enthusiasm and motivation. At the beginning, we have great motivation to achieve something, but this often weakens with time. There exist exercises and aids, however, by which the motivation can be revived and renewed.

Furthermore, there's a need for techniques to handle problems, blockages, etc. None of these is usually offered as part of the usual goal-setting courses.

Unhelpful Self-Help Books

This problem has become more noticeable over the years.

There are thousands of self-help books out there on the market; how many, nobody really knows. Some are good ones, and many are not so good.

Some are badly written: grammatical and spelling errors, poorly constructed sentences, layout problems, etc. abound. All these discourage further reading, even if the content is good.

Many have fundamentally good ideas but give no hints on how to go about following them through. How many contain statements such as: "All you have to do is to change your beliefs"? They then go on to talk about how important this is, without telling you how to go about it. These and similar problems are widespread, perhaps because the authors themselves are unsure how to go about it.

The trouble is, so many of us need a series of clearly written out steps, at least at the beginning. That way, we can be sure that we haven't forgotten or missed anything out.

Lack of courses

My friend Pat Bollag was training as an Alexander Technique teacher. She noticed that none of her fellow students had any idea about how to set goals and achieve their dreams, nor was there anything about this on the course.

Looking around, we discovered that there was nothing useful available anywhere, so we set out to do it ourselves. At first, only the two of us worked on creating something to offer them, adding others later.

Once our materials were finished, we offered the course to the other students. Interestingly, no one was interested. They couldn't see any need for it. Two years later, not one of them was actively teaching, except for Pat. She had, of course, set a goal of having a specific number of clients, which she achieved with little difficulty. The rest, by not setting goals, had no impetus to succeed.

Conclusions

The result of all these problems was the creation of the course (*see above*) and, ultimately, the book you have before you.

I don't expect you to believe everything I say, but ask you instead to try the techniques and methods, and prove to yourself that they're valid and useful. If they don't work for you, you can either tweak them until they do or find other tools that **do** work for you. Not all tools work for everyone every time or we would all have achieved our dreams a long time ago!

> *You shall not accept any information, unless you verify it for yourself. I have given you the hearing, the eyesight, and the brain [mind], and you are responsible for using them.*
>
> Koran 17:36

Why Do We Need Dreams and Goals?

Why Dream?

Without dreams, there is no progress. Even more importantly, without dreams, thoughts and wishes, there is no reality!

Everything that mankind has created and achieved has come from a thought, a dream or a wish in someone's mind. Not only is there nothing new under the sun, there's nothing new if someone doesn't think it beforehand.

The Purpose of Setting Goals

We set goals to concentrate our focus, so that we move in a particular direction.

People often have problems with personal goals for one or more of the following reasons:

- They're overwhelmed by the size of the problem.
- They don't know when they have achieved their goals.
- They have problems with their motivation, giving up at the first sign of problems.
- They have no method of checking whether they're going in the right direction.
- They don't even know what they want.
- They fear they have no dreams.
- They fear discovering that they aren't capable of achieving their dreams.
- They fear success (some people are afraid of success, because it may bring more responsibilities and uncertainty).

Remember: The direction you're heading in is more important than the individual results. Of special importance are the experiences you'll have on the way. Many become upset because they haven't reached their goals and dreams yet. They forget that journeys take time, and that the trick is to enjoy and learn from the experiences along the way. Even miracles take time. This is not the Holodeck!

So find goals and dreams that are **BIG** and *exciting* enough to inspire you!

Why We Set Goals

1. They give our lives meaning and direction. If **we** don't determine the direction we're moving in, others certainly will!

> *The greatest risk is to risk nothing at all.*
> Leo Buscaglia
>
> *If you don't know where you're going, any road will take you there.*
> Lewis Carroll, *"Alice in Wonderland"*
>
> *If you don't know where you're going, you'll end up somewhere else.*
> Yogi Berra

2. They affect the quality of our lives.

To show how powerful dreams can be, I'll use the example of a man who, as a lad at the age of fourteen, had to leave school and work to support his family, because his father had left them. Despite that, this young man had dreams. Among other things, he wanted to be a

- Comedian
- Actor
- Singer
- Dancer
- Diplomat
- Pilot
- Orchestra conductor
- Gourmet chef
- Owner of a sports club
- Doctor

How many of these do you think he achieved?

The answers are on the next page, but please don't cheat and peek.

The lad named David Danny Kaminsky became the man we know as Danny Kaye.

Figure 1: Mystery Man

He achieved the following of the dreams I listed:

✓ Comedian
Not only comedic roles in films, but also as a stand-up comedian and raconteur.

✓ Actor
He had a very successful career with such roles as *Hans Christian Andersen* and the lead character in *The Secret World of Walter Mitty*. He received two Academy Awards.

✓ Singer
He often sang in his films.

✓ Dancer
He danced in films, on stage and even in his own TV shows.

✓ Diplomat
He became an ambassador for UNICEF.

✓ Pilot
He earned his private pilot's licence.

✓ Orchestra conductor
In his later years, he conducted the New Year's concert with the New York Philharmonic Orchestra, which many of the members of the orchestra considered to be the high point of the year.

✓ Gourmet chef
He owned and cooked in a successful gourmet restaurant.

✓ Owner of a sports club
He owned a baseball club.

✗ Doctor
This was the only dream he didn't achieve, although he was allowed on several occasions to observe surgery close up. But considering that laughter is the best medicine, you will see that, in a manner of speaking, he was also a doctor!

In an interview shortly before his death, he stated that he was probably the worst person in the world to be selected to play the role of Walter Mitty. Mitty was a man who constantly dreamt of greatness but was, in reality, a nobody who got nowhere. **He** (Kaye) had achieved almost everything he'd dreamt of doing.

Focusing

Law of Attraction

A great deal has been written, spoken and shown about the Law of Attraction in recent years. We are told about it in such books as *"The Attractor Factor"* by Dr Joe Vitale and *"The Secret"* by Rhonda Byrne, and films like *"The Secret"* and *"What the Bleep?! Do We Know?"*

Simply put, the Law of Attraction states that our most persistent thoughts, whether conscious or unconscious, determine our reality. They attract whatever we consistently think of into our lives: "Like Attracts Like". They also affect how we view the universe.

The principle behind it is that of resonance: energies and frequencies attract similar, compatible energies and frequencies. How the interaction of like frequencies works is best shown by an analogy, using an example from the physical world. Have you ever seen the experiment with a set of tuning forks, two of which have the same frequency? If you rest the ends of them all on a table and strike one of the matched pair, the second begins to vibrate in harmony while the others carry on as if nothing has occurred.

We send out frequencies and energies from our thoughts and the universe responds in kind. Like amateur radio, the universe only receives the frequencies we send, and can only reply with more of the same.

Thus, if we think about abundance, we have abundant lives. If we think about poverty, especially in such negative terms as "I don't want to be in debt all the time" or similar thoughts, we will keep attracting poverty, since that is what we are concentrating on.

What we think about is what the world becomes for us. By changing our thinking, we change our reality. You are shaping your existence with the thoughts you consistently project every moment of your life.

> *Watch your thoughts, for they become words.*
> *Choose your words, for they become actions.*
> *Understand your actions, for they become habits.*
> *Study your habits, for they will become your character.*
> *Develop your character, for it becomes your destiny.*
> Anonymous

So be careful what you think!

Unleash the Power of the Reticular Activating System to Achieve Your Goals

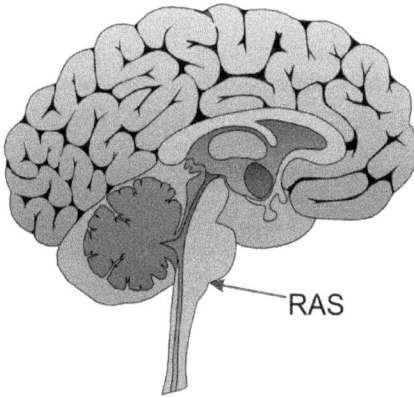

Figure 2: Reticular Activating System (RAS)

Although the actual process is extremely complex, the function of your Reticular Activating System (RAS) is simple and profound: it determines what you will notice, and what you will pay attention to. According to research by Professor George Miller, your conscious mind can focus on only a limited number of elements (7 plus or minus 2 items) at a time, depending on how interesting the subject is to you, and how good you feel at the moment. So your brain expends much effort in deciding what **not** to pay attention to. Countless stimuli bombard you right now; certainly as many as 2 billion per second, perhaps as many as 400 billion, depending on the circumstances. Your brain deletes most of them and focuses on what **you believe are important**. Its mechanism for achieving this is the RAS. Thus, your RAS is directly responsible for how much of reality you consciously experience.

Have you ever bought a new suit or dress, or a car, and then suddenly noticed it everywhere you looked? Why was that? Didn't they exist before? Of course they did, but you notice them now because your purchase of this item was a clear demonstration to your RAS that anything related to it is now significant and needs to be noticed. You have an immediate and heightened awareness of something that has, in actuality, always been around you.

The RAS functions constantly, without any need to be turned on. You must have experienced the *Cocktail Party Syndrome*: you subconsciously hear all the conversations around you at a party.

Only when your name is mentioned, or something that is of particular importance to you is said, do you start to pay attention to a specific one.

This shift in mental posture aligns you more precisely with your goals, outcomes and dreams. Once you decide that something has a priority, you give it tremendous emotional intensity and, by continuously focusing on it, any resource that supports its attainment will eventually become apparent.

Thus, by programming the RAS, you are also telling the Law of Attraction, and, as a result, the whole universe, what exactly it is that you want.

Therefore, it's not crucial to understand exactly how you'll achieve your goals when you first set them. If your dream is to become a millionaire, there are many ways it could happen: an inheritance, a lottery win, being unexpectedly invited to take part in *Who Wants to Be a Millionaire* and answering all the questions correctly, making a windfall on the stock market. The possibilities are endless. So don't limit the "**what**" with a "**how**".

Consider an iceberg:

Figure 3: Iceberg

Less than 10% of the iceberg is visible above the surface, a beautiful analogy for how much of reality is concealed from us. The iceberg explains why the "how" is such a hindrance, because there is so much going on below the surface about which we know nothing.

Trust your brain and the universe to point out what you need to know along the way.

The Power of Focus

What you are paying attention to is what you will experience

How many times have you said or heard: "Seeing is believing," meaning that you would never have believed it if you hadn't seen it? Well, I have news for you: if you don't believe it, you won't see it! Disbelief programs the RAS to ignore the signals that show that something is true, thus reinforcing our belief. This can become a vicious spiral, with the RAS becoming our internal censor, actively preventing us from discovering new things.

There is a lovely section near the beginning of the film *What the Bleep!? Do We Know?* where the inhabitants of the Caribbean islands cannot see Columbus' ships. The Shaman, puzzled by ripples he sees on the water, develops the ability to do so, and shows them how to do it for themselves. They just couldn't believe that ships of such size existed, so they were unable see them.

So, what can't **you** see because you can't believe it?

Unlimited stimulus → unlimited resources and possibilities

The more information we receive that we can process, the more resources and opportunities we can discover and use. The problem is, even under ideal conditions, we still suffer from information overload.

Remember how many stimuli are impinging on you at this moment? Scientists now calculate that there may be as many as 400 billion, every second. That's a lot of incoming information, but the unconscious part of the brain can handle it with ease!

Do you know how many of these bits of information you can pay attention to consciously, every second? Perhaps 2,000. These we put together into larger chunks of information so we can handle them better. Depending on how big the groups of information you can hold together are, they are collected into 7 ± 2 chunks. That's right; you can only hold $5 - 9$ pieces of information in your head at a time! Of course, some of these pieces might have several hundred other bits in them, but probably not much more.

To survive, we must ignore around 99.9999995% of all the information coming to us at any moment, which leads to the next point …

We are creatures of deletion, which is a double-edged sword

We delete from our consciousness everything that we consider unimportant. In fact, it never really gets near the conscious mind at all. Instead, it's stored directly into the subconscious.

However, what we are ignoring may be what is actually important. Think about the times you had an accident of some kind, or missed something important. You were just concentrating on something else and didn't pick up some important clue that things weren't as they should be.

Consider this: how many possibilities for achieving your dreams are you ignoring right now? Fortunately, we have the RAS to help us, but we must tell it what to do.

The subconscious = the decisions we have made, probably early in life

In other words, our subconscious contains our past, including all the deleted information we just talked about. Sometimes this information arises during dreams, but we frequently ignore our nightly fantasies. Usually, it remains in the subconscious, influencing our behaviour in ways we can't guess. The subconscious can be considered to be like a CD or tape player, repeating everything we have taught it, forever and ever.

Unfortunately, because the subconscious is more powerful than our conscious mind, we tend to carry on doing the things we did in the past. It's as if we are on autopilot, with the difference that it can't be turned off. However …

We can make new decisions!

How your life is at present depends on the decisions you made earlier in life. This doesn't mean that you have to continue making the same decisions and carrying on living the same life. It's always possible to decide to do something else. We have infinite possibilities if only we could see them. This book is about helping you find and use some of them.

How about making the decision to change your life, right now?

What we choose to focus on is the reflection of our values and beliefs

The programming of the RAS is not just from our conscious

minds, but much more from our unconscious. All the values and beliefs we hold, both conscious and unconscious, affect what the RAS filters. In turn, the RAS determines what we will focus on, not only because that is what we *want* to focus on, but also because it determines what we will observe and, therefore, be *able to* focus on!

Habitual feelings = habitual focus and questions

If you keep finding yourself experiencing the same emotions, time and again, it's because of the things, people, events and places you habitually focus on (*see the previous entry*). Furthermore, if you keep asking the same questions of life, you'll keep getting the same answers.

Of course, if the emotions are good, upbeat, happy ones, you'll probably want to keep focusing on those things, people, events, places, and questions. On the other hand, the chances are good that you're not so happy with your emotional responses, which is probably why you're reading this book.

People choose what they want to focus on

We choose what we focus on, either consciously or unconsciously, by programming the RAS. In either case, **we** are the ones who choose what is in focus and what we become aware of.

By focusing on positive things, we feel that the world is positive. Negative focus gives rise to negative feelings about the world. And those feelings, being what we focus on, then tell the universe what we want more of, causing spirals of emotion up or down.

How we focus changes how we remember

We can change the way we feel about past events by changing what we focus on as we experience them, and again when we remember them. For instance, if you are at a party, and someone spills a glass of wine on you as you are leaving, what do you remember? Do you remember the great evening you had, with the wine as a little glitch at the end? Or do you remember the wine as the most important part, colouring (!) the mood of the whole memory? You might even remember having the wine stain on your clothes the whole evening! Either way, it doesn't affect what actually happened, only how you remember it, and how you feel about it.

Unsuccessful people remember their failures

Unsuccessful people remember their failures, often larger than life; successful people are the opposite. How do you think about your "failures"? Do you brood about what went wrong? The errors you made? How others got in your way? Are you playing the *Blame Game*?

Unsuccessful people do that.

Successful people give only 20% of their attention to the problem

Successful people spend 80% of their time on searching for a solution, and only 20% on the problem. In other words, they're not "problem solving", they're "solution hunting". They know that there is no failure, only feedback (see page 177).

This is by far a better way of handling "failures". Stop worrying about what went wrong, and start looking for ways to make it right.

Ask yourself positive questions, like

- What can I learn from this?
- How can I take advantage of this sudden change in my life?

Success = "Are you happy with what you are now?"

Read that question again: Are you happy with what you are now?

Please note, I'm not asking whether you're happy with what you have or what you're doing. I want you to ask whether you're happy with who and what you yourself are.

This connects to the presupposition *Attitude is more important than aptitude* on page 199. It's how you feel that's most important of all.

An old cat came across a young cat chasing his own tail.

"What are you doing?" asked the old cat.

"I have decided that my tail represents happiness," replied the young cat. "I am chasing my happiness."

"Ah yes," said the old cat, "when I was your age, I, too, decided that my tail was happiness. I, too, chased my tail, but I seldom caught it. But now I have found that if I go

through life, doing whatever I want, my tail and happiness follow close behind."

Of course, this doesn't mean that you shouldn't go after goals and dreams. If you do, and they are what you really want, happiness will follow, without you having to do anything about it.

> *It is the very pursuit of happiness that thwarts happiness.*
> Victor Frankl, *"Man's Search for Meaning"*

Happiness is an internal state

Happiness really depends on your internal actions and reactions. If, like the young cat, you put the responsibility for happiness on outside things, then they control when and where you will be happy. You have abdicated your responsibility for your happiness and given away your power.

> *The mind is its own place, and of itself can make a Heaven of Hell, a Hell of Heaven.*
> John Milton, *"Paradise Lost"*

I'll tell you a little secret: you can be happy anytime, no matter what the circumstances are! All it takes is a simple decision. Decide to be happy right now!

Personally, I find a genuine smile, even when I'm feeling down, makes me feel better immediately and brings a happier thought to mind, in and of itself. Sometimes, I even find myself chuckling.

That's all it takes.

Why not try it right now? Go and stand in front of a mirror and look at yourself. Try frowning at your image and see how it makes you feel. Now smile at yourself, making the smile as genuine as possible. See if you don't feel much better. Despite what common knowledge says, it does take more muscles to smile than to frown, but it's worth the extra effort!

> *Happiness is the goal of every other goal.*
> Deepak Chopra

Unproductive questions presuppose something that is often not true

If you find yourself asking questions that aren't helping you to get to your goals, maybe you're making assumptions that aren't true. For instance, assuming that people must react in a particular way in certain situations is definitely not true. People have almost infinite possibilities. Expecting them to react that way is only setting you up for disappointment.

Look closely at the assumptions that lie behind your unproductive questions. The best way to do this is to keep asking yourself "Why?" For example, you assume that your lover has to reply, "I love you, too" when you say, "I love you." Ask yourself "Why do they have to reply 'I love you, too'?" Whatever the answer is, question it (for instance, the reply is "because I need reassurance that they love me"). Ask, "Why do I need this reassurance?" Question the answer you get to that question, again and again, until you come to an assumption about reality.

This assumption will probably be a negative belief. Read the section on *Changing Beliefs* on page 173 to discover how to change this into something positive.

Learning

In order to achieve our goals and dreams, we must often learn new ways of doing things, or gather new information to aid us in our decisions.

There are various ways that we learn, as illustrated below.

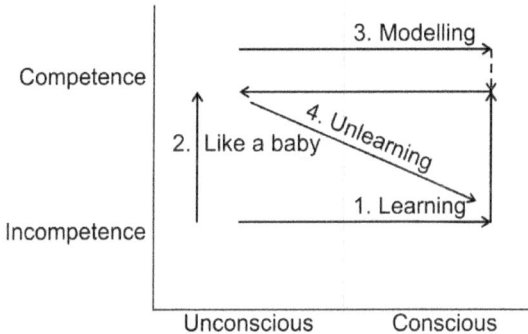

Figure 4: Patterns of Learning

1. Path 1 is the "normal" way. At first, we're not conscious that we don't know something. We're unconsciously incompetent. Later, we become aware of the lack of knowledge and we're consciously incompetent. We then strive to learn what we want to know and gain conscious competence. Eventually, the knowledge has become such an integral part of our being that we're no longer aware that we know it, and are unconscious of our competence. At this point, we have achieved mastery.

   For example, when we are very young, we don't know that we can't drive a car. As teenagers, we become aware that we don't know, and take driving lessons. We struggle with the complexities of shifting gears, signalling, using mirrors, and so on, moving upwards on path 1. Finally, we are so used to driving that we can listen to music or talk to a passenger, all without having to think about when to do what; the knowledge is now classifiable as "unconscious competence".

2. However, there is a second path, where we move from unconscious ignorance to unconscious knowledge or competence, without ever becoming conscious of the learning process or the fact of our incompetence. This can

41

happen at any time, but occurs most often when we are young. After all, we don't know that we can't speak a language, but we learn without ever having the go to school (well, most of us, anyway). It's later in life that such learning moves to path 1.

Phobias are also learnt this way, often in an instant. I know one man whose spider phobia can be traced back to a single event. He woke up one night when he was a young boy. He saw, in the light of a nightlight, a spider hanging on a thread of spider silk only inches above his head. It caused such a fright that he's been afraid of spiders ever since.

3. The third way is to model. Here we bring the unconscious knowledge of the person or persons we are modelling out into consciousness. We then extract the relevant parts, and apply the information to travel on path 1, in order to become competent ourselves. Eventually, the competence drops down into our unconscious. At this point, we can become the models for others. However, in order to be able to teach, we must bring the information back into consciousness ourselves.

4. Finally, there are times when what we have learnt becomes either false or irrelevant. We need to unlearn the old, in order to be able to learn the new.

   This happens more often than we realise. Think about things you learnt in primary school that you had to unlearn in secondary school, because the new information was more relevant, accurate and subtle than the old, only to repeat the process again in university, and again when you started working, and again … ad infinitum. This can be very hard to do at times, and may be a cause of ceasing to learn at all.

The greatest thing of all is that, no matter what your age, any of these paths is available to you. You can still learn, no matter how old you are. I have seen 70-year olds learning to ski and learning well. The old saying, "you can't teach an old dog new tricks" may be true for dogs, but it isn't for human beings!

In the last 10 years, neuroscientists have had to reverse their attitudes concerning learning at advanced ages. Due to a phenomenon called neuroplasticity, we now know that human beings can, and do, reprogram their brains, and the connections within, at any age, learning and unlearning with incredible effect!

> *Learning is not compulsory … neither is survival.*
> W. Edwards Deming

Modalities

A Short Play

Three members of a project management team are meeting to discuss how they want a project to be run from now on, since they have encountered various problems. They are Victor (V), Anne (A) and Keith (K).

V: All right, let's see how quickly we can get a bird's-eye view of what we need to do.

A: I'm all ears.

K: Just as long as we don't sit here 'till lunchtime. I didn't have time to grab anything for breakfast.

A: You're singing my song. I hate long meetings, too.

V: Look here! Stop picturing food, and start focusing on the charts I've prepared.

K: Here we go again! He always has to be one jump ahead of the rest of us.

A: And then he doesn't listen when we tell him something different.

V: Please. I just want to put you two in the picture. It appears to me that there are certain views the users have of the project that we must at least glance at; otherwise the outlook for success is going to be very bleak.

K: So you feel we can put the project back on a firm foundation? If we don't get a handle on **all** their needs, we're going to be skating on thin ice. I take it that they are being woolly and shallow again, not concrete?

A: I've had interviews with their end-users. Listening to them, it's as clear as a bell that they think they've been talking to a brick wall when discussing anything with their IT people. If I can voice an opinion, however, they certainly aren't all talking the same language, even with each other. The IT people just want them to say what they want, loud and clear.

K: And I've been in touch with their IT department. *They* want to start from scratch. On the other hand, I have the feeling that the users are going to try to pressure us to fiddle with the present system. They get uptight when they have to learn anything new hands-on. Which side are we going to support, if any?

V: It's clear-cut to me that the users are a bit shortsighted, because they only have a sketchy idea of the cost of updating such an old system. The IT people probably have the right perspective on that. But I also think that IT is looking through rose-tinted spectacles, because they don't seem to foresee that a completely new system is a horse of a different colour for the users.

K: And neither side is prepared to be the first to lay their cards on the table.

V: Beyond a shadow of a doubt. They don't seem to see eye to eye on anything.

A: And they want us to harmonise the situation?

V: I know I'm painting a very stark picture. But remember, hindsight is always 20:20.

K: Now I'm getting the drift! It boils down to the fact that each side expects us to work hand-in-hand with them, and to give the other side the cold shoulder. If that happens, the project is all washed up before we even have a chance to come to grips with the problems.

A: I'm speechless! Are all these people hearing voices, or what?

K: Could I run out and get a cup of coffee, please? It would make this whole thing a bit more bearable for me, because I'm beginning to find it difficult to follow you both at the moment …

I have a couple of questions for you:

1. Are these people communicating with each other?

2. If not, why not?

The Modalities

Of course, these people have been talking at cross-purposes because each is using a different modality. The modalities are based on our senses, which we use to experience the world, as well as to think. In reality, we all use all of the modalities, unlike the people in the play, who are using only a single modality each. However, one of the modalities will be our preferred method of thinking and handling the world and new experiences; this is our *primary modality*.

Generally, the division of humanity according to their primary modality is:

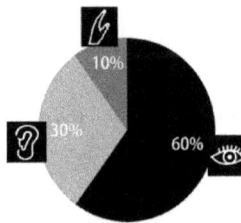

Figure 5: Modalities

For most people, there are three modalities they prefer to use to think: Visual (Victor's way of looking at the world), Auditory (Anne resonates best with sound) and Kinaesthetic (Keith is a "feelings" person). The Olfactory (smell) and Gustatory (taste) modalities as preferred ways of thinking are so rare as primary modalities that they are either ignored or lumped together with the Kinaesthetic.

Examples of modality-based expressions:

"Seeing is believing"	Visual
"I heard it on the grapevine"	Auditory
"I have a bad feeling about this"	Kinaesthetic
"Something smells about this"	Olfactory
"It left a bad taste in my mouth"	Gustatory

With experience, it's easy to discover how people prefer to think. It doesn't enable you to read their minds, but it will help you determine **how** they are thinking; i.e., which modality is active at the moment. If you change the way you breathe, use words like theirs, move your eyes the way they do, mirror their posture, etc., you can change the state of your mind and body to match theirs more closely. This alteration of the way you think by altering your state is called pacing, and can lead to rapport.

> *During the design phase of the major project at the Swiss bank I mentioned in the introduction, I was working with Gery (short for Gerhard), who was the database manager, on the data design. We had sequestered ourselves in a meeting room for a day and a half, and we were getting nowhere.*
>
> *I had assumed that Gery was visually orientated because he insisted on drawing everything we discussed. Since we were obviously talking at cross-purposes, I re-evaluated his communications. It suddenly occurred to me that he kept redrawing the boxes and lines, over and over again. Furthermore, he was using the German equivalents of phrases such as "being concrete", "getting a grip", and "nailing it down", all of which are phrases we use when we're thinking kinaesthetically.*
>
> *I changed my words, body language, actions and thinking to match his, attempting to gain rapport with him, at which point we completed the design in less than half a day.*

The modalities will become important later, but meanwhile, why don't you try to work out what your primary modality is? Below is a table with some indicators of the modalities people use.

Visual

Eyes:	Up or straight ahead	
Vocabulary:	"Perspective", "Clear", "Rosy"	Seeing words
Breathing:	Regular, fast, shoulders	
Voice tone:	High	
Voice tempo:	Fast, in quick bursts	
Muscle tension:	Tensed	
Skin Colour:	Paling	

Auditory

Eyes:	Left and right	
Vocabulary:	"Harmony", "Accord", "Tone"	Hearing words
Breathing:	Variable, in chest	
Voice tone:	Variable, deeper, resonant	
Voice tempo:	Variable	
Muscle tension:	Middling, variable	
Skin colour:	In between	

Kinaesthetic

Eyes:	Down	
Vocabulary:	"Concrete", "Grasp", "Feeling"	Feeling words
Breathing:	Slow, deep, stomach area	
Voice tone:	Deep	
Voice tempo:	Slow, pauses, breathy	
Muscle tension:	Low, relaxed	
Skin colour:	Fuller, flushed	

I'm an auditory person, but I've been practicing the other modalities for years, just so that I can communicate better with the other 70% of humanity…

For more information on modalities, almost any general book about NLP will discuss them.

Logical Levels

NLP trainer Robert Dilts, based on work by Gregory Bateson, created a very useful model of human thinking, the logical levels. This model posits six levels, going from the very concrete (the environment) to the extremely abstract (spirituality).

These levels of learning and change are:

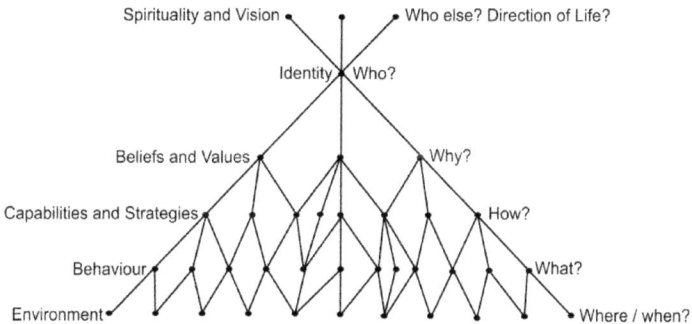

Figure 6: Logical Levels

As you can see, the higher up the hierarchy, the simpler the level is. Furthermore, you can see that parts of each level may connect with more than one part above and below. Connections at the same level have been left out to simplify the illustration. The lowest two levels can be observed directly. The higher levels can only be inferred from the effects they have on the lowest ones.

The higher the level in the hierarchy, the stronger its effects on the lower levels can be. In other words, changing a person's identity will probably have a more powerful effect on their behaviour than changing their capabilities.

The Levels

The levels are interpreted as follows, from the concrete to the abstract:

Environment

This is everything around you: your family, friends, home, work, country, etc. It concerns itself with time, place, people and things. Most of our learning experiences come from here because it contains the whole physical universe. Here we interact with others. It's the context in which the other levels can be seen to be working.

Behaviour

This is the level where we take action, doing and thinking things. All actions are either proactive or reactive; there are no others. Proactive actions come when we make a move towards a goal. Reactive actions are caused either by something in the environment impinging on us, or one of the higher levels being triggered by something we've experienced or believe.

How we behave affects the environment, changing our interactions with others.

Capabilities and Strategies

At this level, we create our behaviours: the skills, talents and strategies we use to get through life. These can either be consciously learned, such as riding a bicycle, or unconsciously, such as learning our native language. In either case, they're now being used unconsciously, and are the basis of our habits, determining what our behaviours are.

Strategies are groups or clusters of behaviours we've put together to handle particular situations: dealing with an overbearing boss, creating relationships with the opposite sex, how we learn, etc.

Beliefs and Values

Here we give ourselves permission to do things, and create the motivation to carry them out.

Beliefs are our convictions that either enable or hinder us, being generalisations about relationships between experiences. They are what we **feel** to be true about ourselves and the world, and are affective (emotional) rather than cognitive (logical). These aren't primarily religious beliefs, although they may be reflected here, but rather our beliefs about reality at a very deep, unconscious level.

There are no "good" beliefs or "bad" beliefs, or "right" and "wrong" beliefs, but only "useful" and "not useful" ones. If the beliefs serve you well and lead to a happy, satisfying and positive life, they're useful. If, on the other hand, they hinder you, then they're definitely not useful.

Please remember that, at some time in your life, **every** belief was useful or you wouldn't have created it. Having created the belief, it allowed you to be unconsciously vigilant, in case the same or a similar situation recurred. Every belief we hold, at some time, helped us survive. Congratulations on having survived for so long! If the belief is no longer useful, it's time to get rid of it, and perhaps replace it with another. NLP and modern psychology have numerous techniques to help you to do this. We'll look at beliefs later, and creating or changing them (see *Changing Beliefs* on page 173).

Values are those things that are important to us; that motivate us to get out of bed in the morning. They're also connected to what's considered socially acceptable behaviour, such as not stealing or murdering.

These two are where we find people's "hearts and minds".

Sometimes, beliefs and values may be in conflict. For example, if you believe that you're a "Plain Jane" or an "Ordinary Joe", but you value friendship, you may find that you still have plenty of friends, despite not being "good looking". It depends on which is the stronger.

Identity

This level contains our sense of self; who we believe we are, separate from the other levels. Here we define the roles we have in life: parent, child, employee, lover, friend, member of the sports club, president of the Women's Club, etc. It's the meeting point of our beliefs and values on the one hand, and our spiritual vision and mission on the other. Since it's the nexus point of our self, changes here can have profound effects on the other levels.

Spirituality and Vision

This is our connection to what's beyond and above us; ourselves in relationship to the rest of the universe. It's the level at which faith, religion and spirituality have their existence. Here we ask questions such as "What is my purpose in life?" and "Why am I here?" Changes at this level can be the most powerful and immediate. We've all heard or read about someone undergoing some profound spiritual experience and becoming an entirely different person as a result. Think Saul on the road to Damascus, or Scrooge on Christmas morning.

I've created another way of viewing the levels, as a series of concentric circles, going from the environment to the core visions of our lives. I often find this useful.

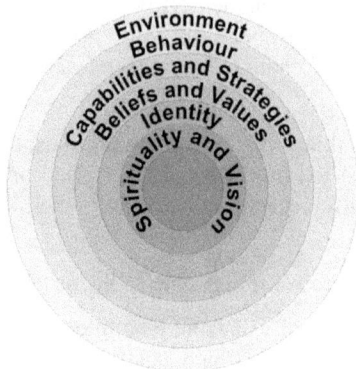

Figure 7: Logical Levels – Another View

An Example

In order to understand the levels better, let's look at some of them using a concrete example.

A man has a drinking problem. Every Friday and Saturday night, he gets falling down drunk with his friends. During the week, he's usually OK, although there may be signs that the behaviour is creeping into his everyday life.

At what level does he have a problem? It could be at one or more of the following. These are only examples because many other causes could also be playing their part.

Logical Level   *Problem*

Environment   The problem might lie simply with the people he spends his time with at the weekend, and the place they meet. If he spends his time with hard-drinking friends in bars but doesn't have the capacity for alcohol they have, keeping up with them drink for drink will be a major problem.

The solution could be as simple as changing his friends or where they meet, although this is probably not as easy as it sounds.

Behaviour	The problem could be that he just doesn't stop drinking. How often have *you* started to do something and kept on doing it, even when it hurt or caused problems?
	A solution might be having another friend come in and take him away for a meal, or home, or something similar.
Capabilities / Strategies	The man might not be capable of realising that he's passed the point of no return. He doesn't realise he's drunk and should stop.
	Here, training the man to recognise the signs that he's becoming inebriated might be a solution.
Beliefs / Values	The man might believe that *real* men work hard, play hard and drink hard. Thus, he has to prove his masculinity by drinking himself unconscious. Statements like "once an alcoholic, always an alcoholic" or "I have to drink to stay calm", are other clear examples of beliefs.
	Here an intervention becomes more difficult because we have to change a core belief held by the man in question.
Identity	This is the level used by Alcoholics Anonymous: "I am an alcoholic." I don't totally agree with this, because it could be creating a belief about identity that isn't true, since the problem actually exists at a lower level. That being the case, they could be making someone become an alcoholic (as an identity), who is, in fact, having problems at one of the lower levels.

Interventions at the level of the problem are possible, and can be very effective. Interventions at a higher level will not only affect the level with the problem, but can cause changes in the person that affect all the lower levels and other parts of their lives. This could be the premise that lies behind the AA system, because it does its work at one of the highest of the levels, whilst appealing to the highest level, spirituality. But I still don't like some of the possible consequences.

As in the example of the AA, people often identify the problem as being on the wrong level.

My Mother has often said "stupid woman" when she did something wrong. I have just as often pointed out that she wasn't stupid (identity), but that she had done something stupid (behaviour). Recently, she's started saying, "I just did a stupid thing", which is a great improvement.

This is important to remember, because it's by this means that we can destroy our children, family and friends, subordinates, etc., making them believe something about themselves that isn't true. Telling a child that they're stupid will, in the long run, make them *believe* that they're stupid, and they may actually *become* stupid. Telling children they're bad, instead of pointing out their bad behaviour, is almost a guarantee of them becoming bad people. Remember, children are born creative and brilliant. Can you learn a new language in less than two years, having had no experience with languages before, or even with learning?

Conflicts

There are two kinds of conflict possible inside a person that can be shown using this model: within levels and between levels.

Examples of conflicts within levels could be:

- Identity Level: Between being a good parent and being a committed employee, or between being a caring giver and being the CEO of a rapacious organisation.

- Beliefs and Values Level: Between the belief that people should be happy and the personal belief that you aren't worthy of being happy.

- Capabilities and Strategies Level: We all have a wonderful mixture of skills and capabilities, which we may not be able to use all (or even any) of the time, which can lead to frustration and stress. If, for example, you have great woodworking and leadership skills, and you want to exercise both at the same time, your career prospects may be somewhat limited.

- Behaviours Level: I'm sure we've all indulged in behaviours that are not in our best interests, such as playing "Minesweeper" instead of finishing off the report the boss wanted an hour ago, because it's more fun …

On the other hand, conflicts between levels could include:

- If you have a vision of world peace (vision), but try to achieve it through rioting (behaviour), there is a major conflict.

- If you think of yourself as a caring, supportive person (identity), but at the same time are sadistic and beat up your wife (behaviour), the conflict is obvious!

- If you believe (beliefs and values) that you should always be honest with others and at the same time have and use an exceptional ability to "put one over" on other people or could sell snow to Eskimos (capability), then there's definitely a conflict.

I'm sure you can think of other examples yourself.

Creating the Dreams

> *The future belongs to those who believe in the beauty of their dreams.*
>
> Eleanor Roosevelt

Now we can start to get down to the nuts and bolts of creating the dreams we want to make reality. To make the process more concrete for you, I'll use the example of the steps I took in order to achieve a particular goal: becoming a certified adult educator. The text will be marked in *like this*. Other examples will be shown in non-italic letters.

Before you start, please print out and use the checklist on the next page, to keep you on track.

Checklist

Item	Done
1. WOW Strategy 1	
2. Writing down your goals	
a. Personal development and health goals	
b. Relationship goals	
c. Career, business, economic and financial goals	
d. Travel, toys and adventure goals	
e. Contribution goals	
3. Setting a timeline	
4. Yes/no decisions	
5. Setting criteria	
6. Converting goals to effective outcomes	
a. Accentuate the positive, present and specific!	
b. Be in control	
c. See, hear, feel, smell, taste	
d. Do? What is the Context?	
e. Ecology check	
7. Being SMART: a checklist	
8. Motivation: reasons for aiming for this goal or dream	
9. Creating the dream	
10. Steps to take	
11. WOW Strategy II	

WOW Strategy I

If I were observing you, how would I know that you'd just succeeded in doing something? Would you do a dance, thrust your fist into the air, shout "Yes!"? Would you clasp your hands to your breast and cry? Would there be other signs, instead?

Think of a success from your recent past (you've had far more successes than you think; otherwise you wouldn't have survived as long as you have). Remember that success and get into the feeling. Write down whatever you did when you succeeded, be it action or word; it must be something that an outside observer can see and hear. Put the paper somewhere you can see it as you carry out the rest of the instructions in the book. On courses, we use shaped pieces of paper and stick them on a pin board.

Whenever you have a success while working through this book, or anything else for that matter, take that feeling of achievement and place it onto the paper (stacking the anchors), like depositing money at a bank. It can be any success, such as finally writing down your dreams, refusing to eat that last piece of chocolate cake in the refrigerator, etc.

The Magic Lamp

When I'm doing this on a course, I then pass around an old oil lamp a friend gave me for the first time I ran the course. I tell the participants to rub the lamp and make a wish. That wish must be a serious one, one that they truly want. Inside the lamp are various small stones. I encourage them to select one. This is a concrete connection to the wish they've just made, a manifestation of its coming reality.

Since I can't give you the lamp to rub, here's a picture of it for you to use. But please, be serious about your wish!

Figure 8: The Magic Lamp

Afterwards, I make a small speech about the lamp:

I hope you've been serious about the wish and made one that truly means something to you, because the lamp really **is** *magical.*

By making the wish, you've woken two genies: a little one and a big one.

The little genie isn't very old. He's only as old as you are. He's not as strong or powerful as the genies that have lived for many centuries. He can only accomplish small miracles. But he knows that even the smallest miracles can make a difference, and that small miracles accumulate until they become big ones. The large miracles may take a little longer to achieve, that's all.

Moreover, he knows that he can call on other genies, even the bigger and more powerful ones, up to and including the most powerful genie of all, to help him. There's no miracle that's impossible to all the genies in the world, unless it's physically impossible for such an event to occur, like turning time backwards.

This little genie is now going to work for you, to create the reality of the wish you have made. Please don't discourage him, or confuse him by changing your wishes. It only upsets him.

The biggest genie can do anything at all, if you give him enough time, and avoid discouraging or confusing him, just as you would with the little one.

The little genie is your subconscious mind. The big one is the whole universe!

Free-Writing

Free-writing is a technique designed to help you release your creative side.

There are two kinds of free-writing: pure and focused.

Pure free-writing happens when you simply write down what's going on in your head at the present moment; it's sometimes called *stream of consciousness writing*. It can be very useful for getting your thoughts in order, or to write down the feelings of an experience in black and white.

Focused free-writing, although similar, has a specific theme or subject. By using free-writing with a particular theme in mind, any associations in your mind have the chance to come out into the open.

The rules are simple:

1. Allot a definite time period for the exercise. 10 minutes is a good place to start, but take half an hour, if that's what you need.

2. Write fast!

3. Once you start writing, don't stop.

4. The direction of writing is from left to right and top to bottom; you aren't allowed to go back to change anything you've written. That comes later, if you wish.

5. Trust the process and accept whatever appears, no matter how absurd, painful, banal or boring it may seem.

The rules apply equally well whether you're writing with pen and paper, or using a computer. They're intended to quieten down and shut up your *Inner Editor*, who constantly wants to edit and change what you've just written. If this doesn't work, then you'll probably need to use a little *Delayed Gratification* (page 169).

We'll be using free-writing for writing down our goals.

Setting Your Goals

- Write down everything that you'd like to improve, achieve or change in your life

- Write down everything and anything you can imagine

- Keep going

- Be silly, be crazy, be a child again

- Discover what it is you really want

- Question: What would I want for my life if I knew I couldn't fail?

- Question: What would I want if I knew I could have it any way I wanted it?

- Keep your pen moving

- You can do it

- What are your innermost dreams?

- Give yourself the gift of inspiring ideas right now

- See your future very, very bright

- Feel really free

- This is really great

- Flow with the music

- You have everything you need to succeed

- Feel really inspired

- You can do it!

Everything you can imagine is real.

Pablo Picasso

Imagine better than the best you know.

Neville Goddard

Getting Started

You'll find questions about goals on the following pages, to help you write down what your dreams are. Think about them, and see which ones start you writing. They aren't a complete list. They're only meant to get you thinking. They are divided into five areas of our lives:

- Personal development and health

- Relationships

- Career, business, economic and financial

- Travel, toys and adventure

- Contribution

Print out or photocopy the goals entry pages following the question pages, or even just take sheets of paper and write the titles on them. Use them to write down your goals.

You don't have to answer all the questions, or even use all of the lists. In fact, when you repeat the whole process, you can go back to your old lists of goals and select a new goal from one of them. However, if you're serious about unleashing your dreams, I would suggest that you go through all the lists the first time round. It's also a good idea to do the whole thing again on a regular basis, because you might discover new goals you'd "never have dreamt of" before, as well as realising that some of the goals are no longer important. You might even discover that your priorities may have changed!

Problems Getting Started?

Sometimes we have problems starting with setting our goals down. It's as if we can't make ourselves believe they're possible. The trick is to bypass our fear of the future and treat everything as if it were in the past, or to give a really powerful reason for writing that list. Here are some suggestions, just to get you started.

The Letter

Imagine you're writing to a close friend exactly one year from today. You haven't seen him or her for a long time, and you want to tell them everything that's happened.

You're looking back at everything that you've achieved in the last year, all the successes, the goals and dreams that have become reality, every good thing that's occurred. Write down the goals you've achieved and the steps you took to get everything done.

The Birthday Party

For longer-range goals, imagine you're celebrating your 60th, 80th or even 100th birthday. All your relatives and friends are gathered around, and your partner or oldest son / daughter / grandchild / friend stands up. They tell the others about what a great person you've been, the fantastic things you've achieved in your life, and how incredibly glad they are to have known you and shared in at least a part of your life. What do they say about you?

The Miracle-Worker

Imagine you've just been told that you have a week to live, no more, but possibly less. How would you feel?

Now imagine that a friend has told you about a miracle-worker who could cure you. How do you feel?

There's a condition attached to the miracle, however: you must start living your dreams and goals. You must make a list of them to give to the miracle-worker, so they know that you're worth saving. Then you must keep your promise.

What would you choose?

I thought you would. Now start writing that list!

Reverse Psychology

How about the times when you can't think of anything positive you want, only the negative things you don't want? You can still create a list of dreams, but it's a three-step process:

1. Write down everything you don't want.

2. Using *Creating Positive Statements: An Exercise* on page 87 as a guide, convert the negatives into positives.

3. Destroy the original negative list (burning is a good way, because it releases the energy back into the universe), and continue with the positive one.

Other Methods of Recording Your Dreams

Of course, not all of us are particularly good at writing down our most private thoughts, dreams and goals. Here are some other possibilities:

- Drawing what we want out of life. It doesn't matter how crude and primitive the drawings are. If they come from the heart, they're a true picture of what lies within us.

- One of the best ways to graphically show our dreams is to combine drawing and writing using Mind Maps. If you use them or have computer software to create them, they're a wonderful way of recording your dreams, because you can show how they're grouped together and how they connect to each other. A good place to start is reading one of Tony Buzan's books on the subject *(*see *Books* on page 221 in the *Appendices*).

- A variation on Mind Maps is Bubble Maps or Bubble Charts. Unlike Mind Maps, they have no specific centre. They consist of bubbles with words or phrases in them, connected to other bubbles by curved lines. They're more useful if you have no central theme but are instead exploring the (often multiple) connections between different concepts and ideas.

- Using a cassette recorder or other medium to record what we dream. Of course, afterwards, it's a good idea to transcribe our words onto paper. Writing out our dreams gives them a feeling of reality that can be achieved in few other ways. It also records what you really want in black and white for the whole universe to see. The pen is truly mightier than the sword!

- For the technically minded, there's also the possibility of using voice-recognition software to dictate your dreams directly into the computer and have it written out. If this is your thing, go for it. Just remember that physically writing something down gives it an immediacy you can't achieve otherwise.

Goals

Personal Development and Health Goals

- What would I like to learn?

- What skills do I want to master in my lifetime?

- What are the character traits that I would like to develop?

- Who do I want as friends?

- How do I want my physical body to look?

- What is my current exercise goal this month, or do I even have one?

- What gets in my way when starting or continuing a balanced health maintenance program?

- What are my target weight, and my plan and time frame to get there?

- How can I improve in getting more sleep?

- What is my ideal overall appearance?

- Would a personal trainer help me develop and reach my goals more effectively and can I afford one?

- Of the meals I eat each month, how can I eat more healthily, and what can I change in order to eat more healthily without getting bored?

- What books can I read and classes can I take to improve my health or upgrade my skills?

- Is it time for me to go in for a complete physical and when was the last one I had?

- How can I reduce or eliminate alcohol, chemical dependencies and/or smoking in my body?

- In what ways may I be able to cook in a healthier manner?

- How can I improve my current heart rate, blood pressure, and cholesterol count?

Personal Development and Health Goals

_____

_____

_____

_____

_____

_____

_____

_____

_____

_____

_____

_____

_____

_____

Relationship Goals

- How can we best nurture our support for one another?

- How will we communicate with one another on a daily basis?

- How dependent will we be toward one another, and is it healthy?

- How can we give our mutual intimacy a boost in the relationship?

- How long do we intend our relationship to last? For example, do we want to marry?

- How will we ensure that we respect each other's rights?

- How will we help one another "grow"?

- How can we keep the fun in our relationship?

- How will we include others in our relationship without losing our support for one another?

- How should or will we approach problems?

- How will we solve problems?

- How are we going to handle various differences of opinion?

- How will we handle irritation with one another and is it worth the effort?

- How are we going to handle fights and bring them to a healthy resolution?

- At what point will we seek help for ourselves if our fighting gets out of hand, or will we even bother? For example, will we seek counselling together?

- Will we agree to disagree?

- How can we ensure mutual growth in this relationship?

- How open are we to taking responsibility, jointly and individually?

- How can we ensure that our individuality doesn't get lost?

- How can we use our unique, individual personalities to help each other and our relationship to grow?

- How open are we to being assertive?

- What steps will we take, if one or both of us begins to feel smothered by the relationship?

- What steps are we willing to take, if one or both of us has the need for mental-health assistance?

- How are we going to promote each other's physical health, and will we be supportive of each other?

- What steps can we take to handle jealousy, a sense of competition, or resentment toward one another?

- How are we going to make time to do all the things we want to do?

- How are we going to arrange our schedules, so that we can pursue our unique, individual interests, and still spend quality time together?

- How free are we to pursue our distinct interests and friends?

- How committed are we to setting up long-range relationship goals and short-range objectives to reach those goals?

- How committed are we to setting up times in which we can nourish one another and keep our relationship on track?

- How can we structure ways to get the "required'" relationship maintenance tasks done?

- How can we delegate the maintenance tasks so that neither of us feels that we are doing too much?

- What place will religion, hobbies, sports and outside interests have?

- How important are those things to our relationship?

- Can we nurture our differences?

Relationship Goals

_____

_____

_____

_____

_____

_____

_____

_____

_____

_____

_____

_____

_____

_____

_____

Career, Business, Economic and Financial Goals

- How much money do I want to earn each year? Do I want to make more money?

- Am I making the kind of money that I want to make?

- What do I want my net worth to be?

- Does money even matter to me?

- Would I like to become a leader in my industry?

- How much investment income would I like to have?

- By what age do I want to achieve financial independence?

- What are my money management goals? Do I need to:

  o Balance my budget?

  o Balance my account?

  o Get a financial coach?

- What investments would I like to make for my future?

- How much do I want to be able to spend on travel and adventure?

- How would I like to contribute to my field?

- What breakthroughs would I like to create?

- Would I like to become a supervisor? Manager? CEO?

- What would I like to be known for in my profession?

- What kind of impact do I want to have?

- Do I want to start my own company?

- Do I like what I'm doing right now?

- What am I passionate about?

- What could I be doing that would make me happier than I am right now? Would I be happier simply switching positions or getting a promotion? Or would I be happier changing careers altogether?

- Why am I still working here? What is stopping me from leaving this job or getting that promotion?

Career, Business, Economic and Financial Goals

_____

_____

_____

_____

_____

_____

_____

_____

_____

_____

_____

_____

_____

_____

_____

_____

Travel, Toys and Adventure Goals

Write down everything you could ever want, have, do, or experience in your life. Be wild and crazy, like a child writing a letter to Santa Claus!

- Would I like to build, design or buy a
  - o dream house?
  - o holiday home or apartment?
  - o designer wardrobe?
  - o music studio?
  - o art collection?
  - o expensive sports car?
- Would I like to see a
  - o London play?
  - o Broadway musical?
- What exotic places would I like to visit?
  - o Would I like to sail around the Greek Islands?
  - o Would I like to meditate in a Buddhist monastery?
  - o Would I like to take a Caribbean or world cruise?
  - o Would I like a season ticket to attend symphony concerts or football games?
  - o Would I like to attend an International Music Festival?
  - o Would I like to attend a Shakespeare play in Stratford-upon-Avon?
  - o How about a Wagner *Ring Cycle* in Bayreuth?

Travel, Toys and Adventure Goals

_____

_____

_____

_____

_____

_____

_____

_____

_____

_____

_____

_____

_____

_____

_____

Contribution Goals

These can be the most inspiring, compelling and satisfying goals of all. This is your opportunity to leave your mark, creating a legacy that will make a difference in people's lives.

- How can I contribute?
    - o Make regular contributions to a charity of my choice.
    - o Arrange a shipment of food, clothing, etc. to Africa or other Third World country, or a disaster area.
    - o Adopt a child.
    - o Support a Third World family with a regular cheque.
    - o Read to the blind.
    - o Volunteer some of my time to a local charity.
    - o Visit a man or woman in hospital.
    - o Use my professional skills to help someone out.
- How can I help to:
    - o Protect the ozone layer?
    - o Improve the quality of the air we breathe?
    - o Clean up the oceans?
    - o Work to prevent global climate change?
    - o Eliminate racial discrimination?
    - o Make someone else's life a little bit easier?
    - o Is it possible for me to create something, some product that has the potential of contributing to the quality of other people's lives?

Contribution Goals

_____

_____

_____

_____

_____

_____

_____

_____

_____

_____

_____

_____

_____

_____

_____

Setting a Timeline

Next to each of the goals and dreams you've written down, try to write how long you estimate it'll take to achieve it. Be as realistic as you can. Things can take longer than you think, but they may also happen much more quickly than you can imagine. Remember: goals are wishes with a deadline.

Below is a diagram showing a nonlinear scale you can use as the basis of your estimation. If you think something will take three months, write "(3M)" next to it. If you want to become a doctor, and you know it takes five years, put "(5Y)" next to that goal.

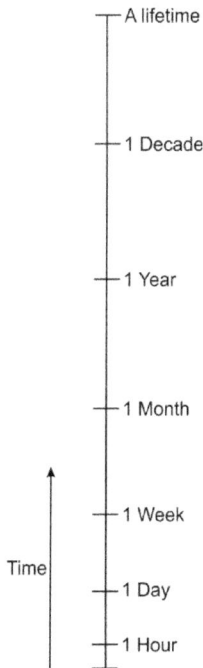

Figure 9: Timeline

For your first try, select one or two goals that will take from a few months to about a year or so to achieve, no more than one from any one class. Use these for the later steps of the process. Next time, you can be more ambitious. If you can't choose which goals to use, try *Yes / No Decisions* below, or *Setting Criteria* after that.

Of course, many goals can't be treated like this, because we have no idea at all how long they could take.

Setting a Timeline

_____

_____

_____

_____

_____

_____

_____

_____

_____

_____

_____

_____

_____

_____

_____

_____

Yes / No Decisions

There are times when we have to decide whether something is right or wrong for us, whether it's a "yes" or a "no". Such decisions are often not amenable to logical processing, but instead are made by "feel". But how do we know when the feeling is right?

If you always know when the feeling is "yes" or "no," and you're always right, you can skip this exercise; it's for people who aren't always sure.

1. Print out the next page, cut it into three pieces, and lay them out in a triangle on the floor, about a yard apart.

2. Stand on the Meta-Position and think of three examples of when you felt "yes" and it proved to be right.

3. Step onto the "yes" position while entering the state of the first of these decisions; see, hear and feel how it was at the time. Imagine you are back at that time, making that decision.

4. Take a small step farther and enter the second of the decisions, again seeing, hearing and feeling how it was.

5. Take a second small step and enter the third of the positions.

6. Return to the Meta-Position and consider what was common to all three; a "feeling" or other signal (e.g., visual) from inside.

7. Can you consciously cause the signal to occur, or is it a response from your intuition, unconscious, etc.?

8. Repeat steps 2 – 7 for "no", when you had a "no" feeling to a decision, and that proved to be the right decision to have made.

9. What's the difference between "yes" and "no"?

Once you've determined how you differentiate yes and no from inside, you can use it to determine whether to follow a particular goal or dream you've written down, or indeed for any other yes / no decisions you make.

Yes / No Decisions

Yes

No

Meta-
Position

Setting Criteria

Remember *Criteria are insufficient* on page 23 in the introduction? There are often personal, subjective and emotional (affective) criteria that have to be taken into account when determining whether goals and dreams have been achieved.

It's necessary not only to determine which criteria must be fulfilled in order for you to have achieved your goals and dreams, but also their relative importance to you, in order of priority. The method shown below can be used for any situation in which you must decide among various criteria, be it deciding how to determine whether a goal has been reached, job-hunting or deciding what you most want in a prospective partner.

The following steps outline a method for learning which criteria are the most important for you (there's an example afterwards, in case the explanation seems too abstract):

1. Print out the Setting Criteria page at the end of the example.

2. Write a list of all criteria you believe must be fulfilled, in order for you to consider that the goal or dream has been achieved. Write down everything of any importance. If you have 7 or more, then you are possibly setting yourself up to fail.

3. Evaluate the hierarchy of the criteria using the following method:

   a. Take the first two criteria, and imagine that you have them each in one of your hands. Identify them as criterion A in the left hand, and criterion B in the right.

   b. Ask yourself: "If I had to decide between a goal in which I had criterion A, but with no chance of criterion B, and a goal in which I had criterion B, but without any criterion A, which would I prefer?" One of them will be the more important to you.

   c. Keep whichever one you prefer, and imagine the next criterion in the other hand. Repeat step **b** with them.

   d. Continue until you have gone through the entire list of criteria; you'll be left with a single criterion that'll be the most important to you.

   e. Write a "1" next to this criterion.

    f. Take the next two criteria on your list, and continue steps **a** through **e** until you've numbered them all.

4. Write the list out on a fresh copy of the Setting Criteria page, in numerical order.

5. Somewhere on that list is a cut-off point (usually after the third or fourth criterion), where the criteria are of lesser importance. If you achieve only the ones above the cut-off, you can consider that the goal or dream has been successfully achieved.

Example

I'm looking for a new job.

I list the criteria I feel are important for me, and which of them must be satisfied if I'm to be happy in the work I'm doing. In no particular order, they are:

1. I must be working together with other people, achieving something that we can't achieve on our own.

2. I want a good salary.

3. It must be something that improves the lives of those for whom it is intended. It either adds something positive, or it lessens or removes something negative.

4. The work must be easy.

5. It must be something new and innovative.

Taking criteria 1 and 2, I ask myself: "If I had to decide between a job in which I worked with other people but the pay is lousy, and a job in which I get great pay, but I would be working on my own, which one would I prefer?" The answer is the first choice, meaning that criterion 1 (working with other people) is more important to me than pay (2). I discard criterion 2.

Taking criteria 1 and 3, I would ask: "If I had to decide between a job in which I worked with other people but it doesn't actually improve anyone's life, and a job in which I do something that improves the lives of others, but I'm doing it on my own, which would I prefer?" I determine that 3 is more important than 1.

After testing criteria 3 and 4, I find that number 3 is still more important. The same occurs comparing criteria 3 and 5.

I write "1" next to criterion 3.

Having already determined that criterion 1 is more important than

2, I can skip testing them again, and go straight to comparing criteria 1 and 4.

Repeating these steps as necessary, I end up with the following list on a fresh page:

1. It must be something that improves the lives of those for whom it is intended. It either adds something positive, or it lessens or removes something negative.

2. It must be working together with other people, achieving something that we can't achieve on our own.

3. It must be something new and innovative.

4. I want a good salary.

5. The work must be easy.

The cut-off point is between criteria 4 and 5, meaning that easy work is not important enough for me to worry about. If the first four criteria are satisfied, but the work isn't easy, I'll still consider the job to be good.

This same method can be used for any choice where there are criteria that are affective (emotional) instead of cognitive (logical).

Setting Criteria

_____

_____

_____

_____

_____

_____

_____

_____

_____

_____

_____

_____

_____

_____

_____

_____

Creating Positive Statements: An Exercise

Before we actually start converting goals to outcomes, which is the next phase, we need to practice converting negative phrases into positive ones. Knowing how to do this will be important during the first step.

Find a positive way of saying the same thing as the phrases below. Example answers are on the next page (no peeking now!).

- I want to lose weight.

- I don't want any more stress.

- I want to stop arguing with my spouse.

- Don't tell me what to do!

- I can't stand it anymore.

- You aren't the person I knew.

- I can't memorise the twelve times tables.

- I love my job, but I can't stand my boss.

- He doesn't give me any credit.

- I don't remember names well.

- Don't forget *to* …

Answers

These are not the only answers, they are simply the ones I came up with. You may find your answers differ greatly. If that's the case, fantastic! The only thing that needs to be right is that the answers are *positive!*

- I want to lose weight.
  I want to be slim.

- I don't want any more stress.
  I want to be calm in stressful situations.

- I want to stop arguing with my spouse.
  I want to communicate positively with my spouse.

- Don't tell me what to do!
  Let me do this my way!

- I can't stand it anymore.
  I want the situation to change.

- You aren't the person I knew.
  You / I have changed.

- I can't memorise the twelve times tables.
  I want to memorise the twelve times tables.

- I love my job, but I can't stand my boss.
  I wish my boss would leave.

- He doesn't give me any credit.
  I want him to give me the credit I deserve.

- I don't remember names well.
  I want to remember names better.

- Don't forget to …
  Please remember to …

Many of these, by the way, wouldn't be good as outcomes, for reasons discussed on the next pages.

Converting Goals to Effective Outcomes

Just as goals are wishes with a deadline, outcomes are "goals on steroids". They inform us how we'll be able to tell when we're close to achieving our goals, and when we've actually got there.

They also help to raise and maintain the enthusiasm necessary to carry on through to the end, by stimulating the emotions.

The goal I chose was to attend courses in order to become a certified adult educator. Having examined the courses offered by various schools, I decided to attend a series of three courses offered by a particular school. Considering when the courses ran, and the time I would have to spend between courses writing the course work necessary (concepts, coaching reports, projects, etc.), plus the fact that I was otherwise working full time, I concluded that the timeline would be about 1½ - 2 years.

With this information in hand, I started on the next steps.

Print out, or photocopy, and use the worksheets for the five steps of this process.

A. Accentuate the Positive, Present and Specific!

Always say what you want, and **not** what you *don't* want. Concentrating on what you don't want only attracts more of the same thing that you already have (Law of Attraction).

Also, on some levels of the subconscious, there's no such thing as a negative; negation only exists in language, not in experience. To illustrate this, consider what goes through your mind when you read the following statement: *"The dog does not chase the cat."* Chances are, for a moment, you had a mental image of a dog chasing a cat before you negated it. This is why children often do exactly what we have told them not to do, because they didn't hear the "don't" or "not".

> *Never talk defeat. Use words like hope, belief, faith, victory.*
> Norman Vincent Peale

It must be in the present tense, as if it's already been achieved, using such language as "I have ..." or "I am ..." Using phrases like "I want ...", "I will have ..." or "I need ..." (this one's a real no-no!) will ensure that you never **get** what you're asking for, but will always **want** or **need** it!

It must be specific, since the universe cannot respond well to fuzzy objectives. The more specific it is, the better because it concentrates your mind on exactly what you want. And we already know that focus activates both the RAS and the Law of Attraction.

Good	*Bad*
I am slim and fit. I weigh 150 pounds.	I want to lose weight.
I am assertive.	I don't want to be such a doormat.
I have a new, fire engine red Jaguar XJS.	I want a new car.

Useful questions:

- Is my outcome stated in the positive? Look for any negative words or phrases. Remember that stopping and losing are negatives!

- Am I writing it as if it is **already** real?

- What exactly do I want?

- Is it possible to achieve this outcome?

- What is the intended purpose of the outcome? What is the payoff?

- What will I have that I didn't have before?

- Can I make a picture of it? What would it look like? (If I can imagine it clearly, I can accomplish it!)

I have successfully completed the three necessary courses and am now a certified adult educator.

A. Accentuate the Positive, Present and Specific!

State your desired outcome in the positive, present and specifically

_____

_____

_____

_____

_____

_____

_____

_____

_____

_____

_____

_____

_____

_____

B. Be in Control

The initiation and achievement of your outcomes must lie in your hands, and not in those of someone or something else. Focus on what you can do, so that you can be responsible for starting and maintaining it. Even if the outcome involves others, you can still choose how you'll behave.

One of the worst traps is when we say: "I'll be happy when ___ [fill in the blank]." You'll never be happy, because your happiness is in the hands of other people and outside events. Even then, achieving your aim will leave you waiting for the next thing to make you happy.

Here is where you make the decision to change your behaviours so that you can gain what you desire.

Good	*Bad*
I am more assertive with my husband when he drinks.	Everything will be all right if my husband stops drinking.

Useful questions:

- What will I do to achieve this outcome?

- Are the behaviours that enable me to produce this outcome under my control?

- What do I need to reach my outcome?

- What will I be doing?

I have successfully completed the three necessary courses.

B. Be in Control

Ensure that you can initiate and maintain your outcome

_____

_____

_____

_____

_____

_____

_____

_____

_____

_____

_____

_____

_____

_____

_____

_____

C. See, Hear, Feel, Smell, Taste

State your outcome in sensory-specific language.

How will you know when you have accomplished your goals? We can only determine whether we've achieved our goals through our senses. Look at your language and be sure that you can identify what you'll see, hear, feel, smell and taste when you get your outcome. Will you be behaving differently? If so, describe that. Put yourself in the picture of your desired outcome, and be sure that you can specifically describe how you know you've accomplished this goal.

What will you see, what will you hear, and what will you feel, smell and taste, that'll tell you that you've achieved your outcome? Describe both yourself and your environment. Insist to yourself on specific descriptions of sensory input or behavioural changes.

Good	*Bad*
I see my bank balance standing at a million, hear the congratulations of my friends, and feel the champagne bubbles going up my nose.	I have a lot of money.

Useful questions:

- How will I know when I've got it?

- What will I see, hear, feel, etc.?

- What will I do that's different?

I see the certificate hanging on the wall of my office, hear the congratulations of the others on the course and of the teachers, and I feel the handshakes and pats on the back.

C. See, Hear, Feel, Smell, Taste

State your outcome in sensory-specific language

I will see _____

_____

I will hear _____

_____

I will feel_____

_____

I will smell _____

_____

I will taste _____

_____

My friends / associates / family will feel _____

_____

My friends / associates / family will say_____

_____

D. Do? What's the Context?

When, where, with whom, etc. do you want to have this outcome (appropriately contextualised)? Be sure to specify the situations in which particular behaviours and goals are appropriate, and those for which they aren't. Identify how you'll know the difference.

Good	*Bad*
I am more assertive with the president of the football club at meetings.	I am assertive all the time. *[What about with your 3-month-old baby?]*

Useful questions:

- When and where do I want this?

- When and where not?

There is no specific context for achieving this outcome, although it does serve as the basis for other dreams to come.

D. Do? What's the Context?

State the context(s) in which you want this outcome

_____

_____

_____

_____

_____

_____

_____

_____

_____

_____

_____

_____

_____

_____

_____

_____

_____

E. Ecology Check

Does the outcome conflict with any major, deeply held beliefs and values that you have? How will it affect your body, your family and friends, your career, the environment, or the world?

Achievement of the goal must not only bring new positive effects into your life, it must also maintain everything positive from before. Check carefully that none of the benefits of the present situation are lost or eliminated.

Good	*Bad*
Helping other people is good / I am a doctor.	Money is filthy lucre[1] / I am a millionaire.

Useful questions:

- What will happen if I get my outcome? How will it affect my life?

- What are the risks? What problems could be caused by the proposed outcome?

- What might happen in other areas of my life?

  o My body?

  o My friends and family?

  o What about at work, or society in general?

- Would achieving this lead to something else for me?

*I believe that teaching others what I know and have learned to be a great good, if it brings them to my level of knowledge and experience. They can then go farther and I can learn from **them**, in mutual support. The more people who know what I know, the faster and easier it will be for all of us to move to a higher level of knowledge and experience. Newton once said, "... If I have seen farther, it is because I have stood on the shoulders of giants." These days, the giants are often the people with whom we rub shoulders. Paradoxical though it may sound, we can all see farther because we can stand on each other's shoulders.*

---

[1] This is a biblical phrase actually meaning, "dishonestly or illegally obtained money".

It also helps if the outcome is perceived as

Possible	→	attainable
Practicable	→	with large outcomes reduced to manageable steps
Precious	→	worthwhile both in itself and in its effects

E. Ecology Check

Check that your outcome is ecologically sound

_____

_____

_____

_____

_____

_____

_____

_____

_____

_____

_____

_____

_____

_____

_____

_____

Being SMART: A Checklist

Before continuing, it's a good idea to check through our outcomes using the SMART matrix. Print out the SMART Checklist and fill it out with the following information.

S	Simple	The more complex your outcomes, the higher the chance that you'll fail.
	Specific	Vague goals are "fluffy" and guarantee failure.
M	Measurable	Measurable in term of sensory-specific descriptions as well as money, time taken, items used, etc., as appropriate.
	Meaningful to you	There must be an emotional component (passion, enthusiasm, etc.), or the goals won't happen.
A	As if now	Act as if you already have it, and your subconscious mind will cause it to occur.
	Achievable	It must be something possible (e.g., becoming rich) rather than impossible (e.g., flying like Superman).
	All areas of your life / ecological	Achieving a goal in one area of your life will cause changes in other areas. Be sure it's not conflicting with your beliefs and values.
R	Relevant	Check for relevance with the rest of your life.
	Responsible	This is where you take responsibility for it happening.
T	Timed	You must set a definite time limit to achievement. But be reasonable about the length.

S   *The outcome is both simple and specific (pass three courses).*

M   *It's measurable (pass / no pass) and meaningful (I enjoy teaching).*

A   *It's in the present tense and achievable, and the skills are transferable to other areas of my life.*

R   *It's relevant (because I still teach), and I believe that teaching is a good thing.*

T   *A time limit of 2 years has been set.*

SMART: A Checklist

S	Simple	
	Specific	
M	Measurable	
	Meaningful to you	
A	As if now	
	Achievable	
	All areas of your life / ecological	
R	Relevant	
	Responsible	
T	Timed	

Motivation: Reasons for Aiming for this Goal or Dream

These reasons give us both the commitment and compulsion we need to carry out the steps necessary to achieving goals. Use the worksheets at the end of this section for writing down the results.

Ask yourself the following 5 questions:

1. What will I gain?

There is always a gain to be made by achieving goals and realising dreams, or they wouldn't be worth the effort. Is it satisfaction? Or perhaps the feeling of security that comes from having an independent income? Whatever it is, find out what it is and write it down. Remember that the ultimate reason for doing something is **always** that it makes you feel happy.

If you don't know why you want something, you'll never find the enthusiasm to go after it.

Question: What is important to me about this outcome?

I will have new knowledge, which will extend my teaching capabilities. On the other hand, I'll have confirmation that I've already been teaching in a valid manner.

2. What will I miss out on by not achieving (or even trying for) it?

This is the flip-side of question 1. What will you miss out on? It's not just that you're not achieving the goal and the gain that goes with it. It's also the things you'll learn and experience along the way. You could be robbing yourself of something unbelievably good and valuable.

Question: What will I be missing out on?

I'll miss out on new techniques and methods that could improve the quality of my teaching. Also, a certificate is necessary in order to be able to teach at some of the institutions in Switzerland.

3. What will be the cost of achieving it?

Every goal and dream you follow will cost you something, be it money, relationships, energy, time, beliefs about yourself, or something else.

> *I remember during my training as a Reiki Master, as well as having to pay for the training, I had to give up many beliefs about justice in the world. It was (literally) a very painful experience for me, because the rage at the injustice I saw had been stored in my liver, and its coming out was agony.*

You should sit down and consider what the costs are going to be, then decide whether the gains are worth the costs (see *Yes / No Decisions* on page 81). If the answer is "yes", go for it! If the answer is "no", then you can put it aside without regret, relegating it again to a mere wish.

Question: Is it worth the price?

> *It will cost me approximately 10,000 Swiss Francs for taking part in the courses, plus around 7 − 8 weeks course time (to be taken out of my holidays and overtime compensation), plus at least one week of my spare time for completing the various reports, projects and other course material I have to hand in after completing each section. I may also have to change the way that I teach.*

Happy are those who dream dreams and are ready to pay the price to make them come true.
Leon J. Suenes

---

4. What is the cost of not achieving it?

If you don't achieve your goal, what will it cost you? At best, you will remain stuck in the situation you are in now. At worst, things could go downhill, and you will suffer far worse than if you had gone for it.

Question: What will happen if I don't reach my goal?

> *I'll continue teaching the way I have been until now, while being uncertain whether I'm doing it the best way possible. Furthermore, if I have no certification, certain possibly lucrative schools may not be available.*

Life is like a shark. Either you're going forwards, or you're dead.
My late friend Dennis

---

5. *What secondary gain do I have for not achieving it?*

There's often a reason we haven't achieved our dreams: the so-called *secondary gain*. This is something we have **because** we haven't changed. We view it as a thing that gives us an advantage, and are therefore reluctant to give it up.

> *A woman kept having attacks of paralysis of both legs. Although it was painful for her, and meant that her husband had to look after her, it had the advantage of keeping him at home, instead of having affairs with women at work. After all, his self-image wouldn't allow him to be such a rat as to go out and have fun while his wife was so ill at home!*

What advantages do you have for being stuck in the present situation, instead of going out and following your dreams? Are you getting sympathy for being *Poor Me*? How about avoiding responsibility for any changes that happen? Or are you using the fears and hopes of others because you "don't want to upset them"?

Can you find another way to satisfy those needs while achieving your dreams?

Question: What do I get out of my present state that is positive?

Question: How, specifically, will I maintain those things with my new outcome?

> *If I don't learn new methods and techniques, I won't have to improve my teaching, and therefore won't be measured against a higher standard, which I fear I might not be able to achieve.*

Reasons are the "why" of goal setting. Without a "why" there's no success because it always outweighs the "how". "Whys" are the triggers for the emotions that drive us to succeed at what we want to achieve.

Motivation: Reasons for Aiming for this Goal

1. What will I gain?

_____

_____

_____

_____

2. What will I miss out on by not achieving (or even trying for) it?

_____

_____

_____

_____

3. What will be the cost of achieving it?

_____

_____

_____

_____

4. What is the cost of not achieving it?

_____

_____

_____

_____

5. What secondary gain do I have for not achieving it?

_____

_____

_____

_____

Emotions

If you don't bring your emotions into play, you'll get nowhere. Your emotions are the fuel that powers your achievement. They drive you. Become enthusiastic about your goals and dreams, and you'll get there. Treat them with a "yeah, whatever" attitude, and you'll stay where you are.

Remember, emotion can be written as e-motion, meaning energy in motion!

But …

Be careful of falling into a subtle trap: *expectation*. Be enthusiastic about your dreams and keep an attitude of expectation, but don't cling to your expectations. Expectation, if you can't let it go, is betting your happiness on the goal or dream being achieved *exactly* as you've visualised it. It's as if you say: "If it doesn't happen precisely as I want it to, I'll be unhappy!" In that case, the following equation applies:

Expectations = Disappointment

For example, if you have an expectation of $1,000,000, getting only $999,999 will disappoint you, because you haven't achieved your expectation. Or you meet the partner of your dreams, but are disappointed because they're blonde instead of being a redhead.

In other words, you're deciding that the outside world is responsible for your happiness (see *Happiness is an internal state* on page 39). Clinging to your expectation is putting a great emotional burden on your achievements being exactly as you've decided they must be.

Creating the Dream

Print the next worksheet and write down the outcome you've chosen, which will become your dream. Make it as specific as possible. At the end, add the sentences: "This or something better" and "Be it to the highest good of all concerned".

Adding the first rider ensures that we don't limit the possibilities because we might otherwise prevent events and results from occurring that we would "never have dreamt of". It's also an excellent antidote to expectations (*see the previous page*).

The second guarantees that we aren't selfish and that we can dream with love for our fellow beings and ourselves. Also, being a millionaire might not be the greatest good for you and your family.

Of course, this all assumes that you mean what you say and write.

Next, describe how you'll know that you've achieved that dream, describing it using all the senses. Write down what you'll see, hear, feel, even taste and smell, if appropriate. Make the description as intense as possible, using lots of adjectives.

Date and sign it. After all, you're making a contract between you, yourself and the universe!

Now close your eyes and imagine it with all your strength, adding the emotions you'll feel when you have achieved it.

However, when starting, make sure that you can see and hear yourself in the picture.

> *One man forgot that important step; he wasn't in the picture. Everything occurred as he visualised it for his family, but he wasn't there when it happened. He had died of a heart attack achieving it for them.*

Once it is as intense as possible, step into the image and see, hear, feel, etc. exactly as if you were in the scene itself. Enjoy yourself, and enjoy the feeling of having achieved your dream! To make it even more powerful, add new details every time you visualise it.

Do this every morning just after you've woken up, and every evening just before going to sleep (see *Rehearsals* on page 151), and you'll be amazed at how quickly things begin to happen.

By bringing your emotions into play, you're making yourself ever more enthusiastic about your dream. The more emotional energy you put into it, the more power you give it (see *Emotions* above).

Creating the Dream

Write down the outcome you have chosen, which will become your realisable dream:

_____

_____

_____

_____

_____

_____

_____

Describe how you will know that you have achieved that dream, describing it as an outcome:

I will see _____

_____

I will hear _____

_____

I will feel _____

_____

I will smell _____

_____

I will taste _____

_____

Date and place: _____

Signed: _____

Steps to Take

> *By failing to plan, you plan to fail.*
> Benjamin Franklin

These are what Mike Dooley calls the "cursed hows". Setting steps and clinging to them can be a means of limiting our dreams and ourselves, so this part is to be used with the utmost caution. If you've no idea how to achieve your dreams, or don't wish to limit yourself, skip down to point 3 below; your job is to define the "what", and the universe will take care of the "hows".

1. For some dreams, you'll know fairly accurately what you have to do to achieve them. For instance, studying to become a doctor requires that you've finished high school and college. If possible, estimate how long each step will take, as you did for the goals themselves. You can even set actual deadlines if that's what you need. Whatever the steps are, print out the form below, write them down on it, and tick them off as you accomplish them.

1. Other dreams will require a specific set of steps, but you aren't sure what they are. Here's a tip to make things easier. Act as if you've already achieved your dream (see *Acts of Faith (Acting "As If")* on page 154). Think of the last step you have to take to realise your dream. Write it down, with the number "1". Then think about the step you have to take before that one, in order to be able to take that last step, numbering it "2", and so on. Sometimes it's easier to list things backwards because then it isn't so daunting. You're only working out the step necessary to get to the next step. Tick them off as you achieve them (they'll be in reverse number order), and you'll feel that you're counting down to your dream!

2. *The last few steps, as they appear in reverse order:*

   i. *Hang the certificate on the wall of my office at home.*

   ii. *Go to the celebrations for those who passed the course, to receive my certificate.*

   iii. *Complete the concept, using the materials I gathered during the third part of the course, and send it in for evaluation as course work.*

> iv. *Attend the third part of the course, selecting a concept to write and gathering the materials that will be used to write it.*
>
> v. *Etc., ...*

3. Many others, if not most of the dreams, will be in the laps of the gods and the universe, because you've no idea how they'll come to fruition.

Steps to Take

Make a list of all the steps that you can think of right now, that could move you closer to your dream. Put down anything and everything that could conceivably help you achieve this dream.

_____

_____

_____

_____

_____

_____

_____

_____

_____

_____

_____

_____

_____

_____

> *God helps those who help themselves.*
> Benjamin Franklin, *"Poor Richard's Almanac"*, 1757

These steps can also be regarded as micro-goals, milestones or way marks.

Breaking the task down into manageable steps makes it less daunting. If the steps are small enough, they'll seem almost trivially easy, and the goal will be achieved before you know it.

> *Q: How do you eat an elephant?*
> *A: One bite at a time.*

There are times, of course, when you suddenly see a step to take you haven't written down. It comes to you in a flash, or you suddenly hear it or have a hunch. Follow that step. It's "inspired action", a message from your subconscious, the universe, or God that helps you make the journey quicker and easier. It can even save your life.

Two quick examples:

> *I was on the way home from visiting a friend. Driving through the city, there was a part of the trip that required me to turn left on one of three roads. My usual habit was to take the first turn, which then swung to the right, crossing the second road, with the third merging in a short distance later. This evening, I went straight on. As I approached the second turning, I was wondering why I hadn't made my usual choice. Looking to my left while waiting at the traffic lights, I realised that there had been an accident at the junction of the first and second roads, which would have delayed my journey. I couldn't have seen the accident from the first turning.*

> *The second was even stranger. I was on the way home after having signed a contract with my teachers to become a Reiki Master. As I drove along, I kept noticing that the speed would drop from 120 km/h, the speed limit, to around 102 km/h. Even when I accelerated, I would find the speed reducing itself again. Then I realised that it had been raining on the stretch of road I was approaching, which had been dry on the way there. Suddenly, the steering went mushy, and I found myself*

almost aquaplaning. If I had been travelling at full speed, I would have lost control of the car, quite probably crashing it. The interesting question is: how did my subconscious know the road conditions ahead?

Make a list of all the steps that you can think of right now, to move you closer to your dreams. Make a separate list for each dream. Put down anything and everything that could conceivably help you achieve that dream. They don't have to be in order; that can come later, if you feel it's necessary.

> *For all sad words of tongue and pen, the saddest are these, "It might have been".*
> John Greenleaf Whittier

Old Jacob went into the synagogue to pray.

"Yahweh, hear me," he called.

"YES, JACOB," came a Voice out of the heavens. "WHAT DO YOU WANT?"

"Yahweh," replied the old man, "I'm no longer as young as I once was, and I'm worried about the future. When I'm gone, how will my beloved wife survive if she has no money?"

"HM, THAT IS A PROBLEM," admitted the Voice. "WHAT DO YOU WANT ME TO DO ABOUT IT?"

"Yahweh, please help me win the lottery," pleaded Jacob.

"THAT WILL BE NO PROBLEM. I WILL DO AS YOU ASK."

A week went by, and Old Jacob went back into the synagogue.

"Yahweh, it's been a week, and I haven't won the lottery," he moaned. "I don't think I've much time left."

"JACOB," said the Voice, "PLEASE HAVE PATIENCE."

Another week went by, and still no lottery win. Jacob went back to the synagogue.

"Yahweh," he called out. "Why haven't you answered my prayers?"

"JACOB," said the Voice, sounding exasperated, "PLEASE MEET ME HALF-WAY ON THIS. BUY A LOTTERY TICKET ALREADY!"

In all cases, however, there'll be at least one step you can take, just to prove to yourself and the universe that you're serious and committed. If you want a new sports car, how about buying yourself a pair of suede driving gloves, or a special polishing wax? If you want to have a million in the bank, open a special account at the local bank. If you want to be an artist, buy paints and brushes, and enrol in night classes. I'm sure you get the idea.

> *A journey of a thousand leagues begins with but a single step.*
>
> Lao Tzu

Learning from Lao Tzu, the journey can be accomplished by taking the next relevant step, one step at a time, without knowing what lies ahead, as long as the final destination is clear. It's like driving in fog. You know where you're going, so you just keep following the edge of the road until you get there.

> *It had long since come to my attention that people of accomplishment rarely sat back and let things happen to them. They went out and happened to things.*
>
> Leonardo da Vinci

So, no matter how small it is, take that first step now. Please!

Living the Dreams

Once we've started down the path to achieving our dreams, we may encounter stumbling blocks, obstacles and hindrances; this is simply the nature of the world, and there is little we can do to prevent it.

> *Obstacles are those frightful things you see when you take your eyes off your goal.*
> Henry Ford

However, just because we're having trouble moving forwards is no reason to give up, although many people use it as an excuse. This section contains several tools that will help you find your way and maintain your motivation to carry the dreams through to the end. It helps you align yourself with your self, to find the resources you need to succeed, to deal with blocks and lack of motivation, and even shows a way to create new options and ideas.

> *Obstacles can be stepping stones or stumbling blocks.*
> Anonymous

Alignment of the Logical Levels

Often, one of the reasons we can't achieve goals and realise dreams lies in the fact that some of the *Logical Levels* (page 49) are out of alignment with one another. As a result, we are in conflict with ourselves, and our energies are scattered and/or consumed in internal fighting.

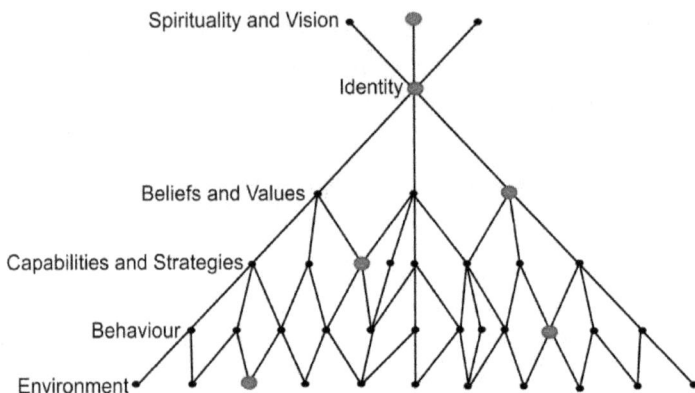

Figure 10: Logical Levels – Out of Balance

If we have all the levels in alignment with one another, then our energies can all flow in the same direction, and we can achieve miracles.

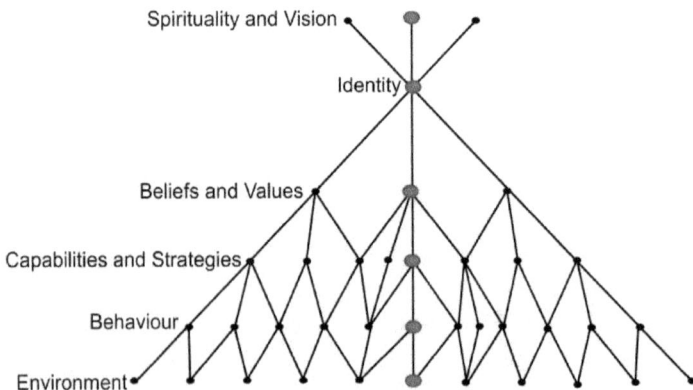

Figure 11: Logical Levels – In Balance

Using the following steps, we can achieve this alignment. There's an example afterwards if the instructions appear to be too abstract.

1. Decide on the goal you want to align yourself around.

2. Physically lay out one space for each of the logical levels. Print out the work materials at the end of this section, cut them into six pieces, and lay them out on the floor one pace apart.

3. Move to the first space, *Environment*, and answer the question: "When and where do I want this goal?" Get a real feeling about this, visualising it as precisely as you can.

4. Move to the second space, *Behaviours*, and answer the question: "What will I do when I'm achieving this goal?" Again, get the feeling for this level, as you must for every level.

5. In the third space, *Capabilities / Strategies*, answer these questions: "How will I carry out these behaviours?" and "What capabilities, skills and strategies do I have or need, in order to carry out those actions in those times and places?"

6. On arriving in the fourth space, *Beliefs / Values*, answer these questions: "Why will I use those particular capabilities and strategies to achieve those goal activities?", "What values are important to me when I am acting this way?" and "What beliefs guide me when I am acting this way?"

7. The questions for the fifth space, *Identity*, are: "Who am I as a person achieving this goal?" and "What kind of person am I?"

8. In the last space, *Spiritual*, answer these questions: "Who else am I serving in achieving this goal?", "What is my mission in achieving this goal?" and "What vision am I pursuing or representing?"

9. Anchor the state that you entered into in the *Spiritual* space (connect it to a little signal you select, such as pressing a particular spot on your wrist, or closing our fist in a particular way). You may find that a visual image or metaphor will spontaneously appear that represents this space for you.

10. Turn around and take the feelings, the inner experience, and the metaphor (if one appeared) and step back into the *Identity* space so that you experience both spaces at the same time. Notice how this enhances or enriches your initial representation of the identity experience, expanding it. Anchor both states together with the same signal, stacking them together. Continue this stacking at each step.

11. Take your experience of both your vision and your identity and bring them into your *Beliefs / Values* space. Again notice how it enhances or enriches your initial representation of your beliefs and values.

12. Bring your vision, identity, beliefs and values into the *Capabilities / Strategies* space. Experience how they strengthen, change or enrich the capabilities and strategies you experience within yourself, or even show you new ones to develop.

13. Bring your vision, identity, beliefs, values, capabilities and strategies into your *Behaviours* space. Notice how even the most insignificant-seeming behaviours are reflections and manifestations of all the higher levels within you.

14. Bring all the levels of yourself into the *Environment* space and experience how it is transformed and enriched.

15. Think of a time in the near future, when you want to apply all of the levels you've just aligned. Take a step forward, move into that future time, and experience as fully as possible how it will be, seeing, hearing and feeling as strongly as possible.

It's a good idea to have someone guide you through the experience for the first few times, to help prevent yourself from mixing the logical levels.

An Example

1. I decide that the goal I wish to align myself around is teaching NLP.

2. I lay out the paper pieces and stand in front of the first piece.

3. I move into the first position, *Environment*, and answer the question with "this will be when I am teaching NLP techniques."

4. In the second position, *Behaviours*, the answer is "I'll be teaching all that I know."

5. The answer in the third position, *Capabilities / Strategies*, is, "I'll be using the skills I have learnt as an adult educator."

6. In the fourth position, *Beliefs / Values*, I answer, "teaching is good."

7. For the fifth position, *Identity*, my answer is "I'm a knowledgeable teacher."

8. In the last position, *Spiritual*, I have a small vision. I see myself as being of light flying over a darkened landscape. I illuminate the darkness below me and behind me, and the light spreads out to the sides. I realise that I am a Lightbringer, a being who is blessed with the ability to bring the light of knowledge into the darkness of ignorance. This is the vision I take with me on the return journey through the Levels.

9. I anchor the state by putting pressure on the webbing between my thumb and forefinger on the left hand, pinching the flesh lightly.

10. I move back into the *Identity* space, when my answer changes to "I'm a nurturing and supporting teacher, imparting the knowledge that the student truly needs."

11. Moving back into *Beliefs / Values*, I answer, "If you can teach, you're duty-bound to do so in the most nurturing manner possible."

12. In *Capabilities / Strategies*, I see that I must be capable of teaching from the heart as well as from the head.

13. In carrying all my experiences into *Behaviours*, I find that the visualisation of me teaching is both gentler and yet more profound.

14. At the *Environment* level, I realise that this extends to all my teaching, not only NLP techniques, but also computer education and teaching Reiki.

15. As I step into the future, I feel how different my teaching will be and how much more effective the imparting of knowledge will become.

Alignment of the Logical Levels

Spirituality

Identity

Beliefs / Values

Capabilities / Strategies

Behaviours

Environment

Development of Qualities, Skills and Resources

Goals and outcomes are simply tools to concentrate our focus and move us in a particular direction.

One reason we really pursue goals and outcomes is to cause us to expand and grow. Achieving goals and outcomes by themselves will never make us happy in the long term; it's who we become, as we overcome the obstacles necessary to achieving our goals that can give us the deepest and longest-lasting sense of fulfilment.

In order to overcome these obstacles, we need to develop:

- Qualities: These are personality traits, beliefs and values within us

- Skills: These are the new abilities we need to develop, new ways of doing things, and new things that need doing

- Resources: Here are resources that may be outside us, which support us in our endeavours. They include such things as money, equipment, people, places, things to be done, etc.

So, questions you and I need to ask are:

- What are the qualities, beliefs and values I need to nurture, develop, change or replace within me, in order to achieve all I want?

- What skills and abilities do I need to develop or extend and enhance?

- What resources will I need? (See *Individuals have all the resources necessary to make any desired change* on page 185 and *People are your greatest resource* on page 186)

Print out the next page and write the list down. If necessary, make sub-goals and way marks out of them.

Development of Qualities, Skills and Resources

- What are the qualities I need to nurture in myself, in order to achieve everything I want?

- What skills do I need to develop?

- What resources will I need?

_____

_____

_____

_____

_____

_____

_____

_____

_____

_____

_____

_____

_____

_____

Using Submodalities to Aid Motivation

Overview

Remember the little play about *Modalities* (see page 44)? Well, the modalities can be fine-tuned, to allow us a more refined experience of the world.

Submodalities reflect how we organise our experiences. At the level of form or process, the difference between a problem state (e.g., unmotivated) and a resource state (e.g., motivated) is to be found in the submodalities of these representations. In other words, submodalities tell us how to feel about the states.

> *On an NLP course I attended, I helped a young woman called Bobbie discover how to determine whether a memory was real, or the result of very intense fantasy thoughts, such as dreams or daydreams. "Real" memories had no frame and faded out to the sides, while "false" one had a definite black frame around them resembling a porthole on a ship.*

Shifting and changing submodalities creates a different perspective. The basic sequence consists of determining the submodality differences between a problem state and a resource state, then "mapping across" from the one to the other to transform the problem state into the resource state.

Problem state	←→	Resource state
Difficult	←→	Easy
Bored	←→	Enthusiastic
Confusing	←→	Understanding
Unsatisfying	←→	Satisfying
Uncompelling	←→	Motivating

Instructions

1. Print out the charts below.

2. Think of something you're highly unmotivated to do **(a)** and something you're highly motivated to do **(b)**. For **(a)**, make sure it's something you are unmotivated to do, or something you hate but have to do. Furthermore, choose **(b)** to be something similar to **(a)**. If **(a)** is motivation about something to do with people, **(b)** should also have to do with people; if **(a)** is to do with career, **(b)** should have something to do with career, etc.

3. Access the unmotivated state **(a)** (get into the feeling, thinking of what you see, hear and feel while in this state). Sometimes, the easiest way to get into the state is to imagine how you'll feel, the next time you're in this situation. Or, if that doesn't work, how did you feel, the last time this happened? For each of the entries on the chart, note down how the unmotivated state looks, sounds and feels. Please note, not all of the entries may be applicable, especially pain-related submodalities.

4. Once you've completed the list, break state (stand up, jump around, sing a silly song, whatever you feel like doing). Just make sure that you're no longer feeling like the unmotivated state **(a)**.

5. Access the motivated state **(b)**, and note down each of the submodalities, as in step 3.

6. Break state again.

7. Compare each of the entries on the list with its opposing partner. Some will be the same, others noticeably different. Note the differences and describe how they are different (e.g., one may be larger than the other; one may be dim and the other bright; one may have sound, the other not; one may be a slide, the other a movie; one might be in colour, the other in black & white; etc.).

8. When you have at least two differences, access the unmotivated state and start "adjusting" the submodalities of the unmotivated state to those of the motivated state. Imagine that you're adjusting the controls on a very complicated TV or stereo.

9. Check whether you now feel motivated about the thing you were previously unmotivated about. If these shifts haven't transformed "unmotivated" to "motivated", go back to step 7 and find more differences.

10. Once you've made the transformation, pat yourself on the back. Congratulations!

This exercise can be used to change any one of a pair of opposites into its opposite: embarrassment into acceptance, fear into courage, or hatred into love, for example. Be warned, the reverse route is just as easy (it's how people fall out of love)!

Using Submodalities to Aid Motivation

	Unmotivated (Problem) State	Motivated (Resource) State
Visual (Images)		
DISTANCE OF IMAGE (very near to very far)	_____	_____
DISTANCE OF OBJECT(S)	_____	_____
LOCATION (front, right, left, up, etc.) – *point to it*	_____	_____
SIZE (very big to life-size to very small)	_____	_____
SIZE OF CENTRAL OBJECT(S)	_____	_____
SHAPE (square, rectangle, etc.)	_____	_____
SCOPE (framed or panoramic)	_____	_____
BRIGHTNESS (bright to dim to dark)	_____	_____
COLOUR (intense to pastel to B&W)	_____	_____
PARTICULAR COLOUR	_____	_____
INTENSITY OF COLOUR / B&W	_____	_____
CONTRAST (high to low)	_____	_____

	Unmotivated (Problem) State	Motivated (Resource) State
DEPTH (flat to 3D)	_____	_____
MOVEMENT (slide vs. movie (with speed))	_____	_____
CLARITY (in focus to fuzzy)	_____	_____
FOCUS (intermittent / steady)	_____	_____
SPECIFIC FOCUS (any particular object(s))	_____	_____
NUMBER OF IMAGES / SHIFTS	_____	_____
VIEWPOINT (from above, below, to one side, etc.)	_____	_____
ASSOCIATED / DISASSOCIATED (are you in the picture or not)	_____	_____
SPECIAL TRIGGER (anything else triggering strong feelings)	_____	_____

	Unmotivated (Problem) State	Motivated (Resource) State
Auditory (Sound / Words)		
SELF / OTHERS	_____	_____
CONTENT	_____	_____
HOW IT'S SAID	_____	_____
LOCATION (left, front, back, etc.)	_____	_____
MOVEMENT (still, moving around)	_____	_____
DIRECTION (inward / outward)	_____	_____
DISTANCE (very near to very far)	_____	_____
TONALITY (high to low pitch)	_____	_____
TEMPO (fast, slow, variable speed)	_____	_____
TUNE (is there a tune? If so, what is it?)	_____	_____
INFLECTION	_____	_____
EMPHASIS OF CERTAIN WORDS / SOUNDS	_____	_____
RHYTHM (even, variable, cadenced, pauses)	_____	_____
CONSTANT OR INTERMITTENT	_____	_____

	Unmotivated (Problem) State	**Motivated (Resource) State**
VOLUME (very soft to very loud)	_____	_____
STEREO / MONO	_____	_____
HARMONY / CACOPHONY	_____	_____
DURATION	_____	_____
UNIQUENESS (gravely, smooth, etc.)	_____	_____
WORDS SPOKEN	_____	_____
SPECIAL TRIGGER (anything else triggering strong feelings)	_____	_____

	Unmotivated (Problem) State	Motivated (Resource) State
Kinaesthetic (Feelings / Sensations)		
LOCATION (whole body or part)	_____	_____
INTERNAL / EXTERNAL (surface)	_____	_____
GOING INTO BODY / GOING OUT	_____	_____
EXTENT (concentrated to spread out)	_____	_____
SHAPE (precise or vague)	_____	_____
SHAPE / SIZE CHANGE	_____	_____
PRESSURE (slight to intense)	_____	_____
TENSION (very rigid to relaxed)	_____	_____
TEMPERATURE (icy to hot)	_____	_____
HUMIDITY (moist to dry)	_____	_____
TEXTURE (smooth to rough)	_____	_____
RIGID / FLEXIBLE	_____	_____
VIBRATION / STILL	_____	_____
WEIGHT (light to heavy)	_____	_____

	Unmotivated (Problem) State	Motivated (Resource) State
DENSITY (light to dense)	_____	_____
MOVEMENT (still or moving)	_____	_____
STEADY / INTERMITTENT	_____	_____
BREATHING (quality; start / end)	_____	_____
INTENSITY	_____	_____

Pain

TINGLING	_____	_____
HOT / COLD	_____	_____
MUSCLE TENSION	_____	_____
SHARP / DULL	_____	_____
PRESSURE	_____	_____
DURATION	_____	_____
STEADY / INTERMITTENT	_____	_____
LOCATION	_____	_____
MOVEMENT	_____	_____
SPECIAL TRIGGER (anything else triggering strong feelings)	_____	_____

The Bridge: The Movement That Connects

Sometimes we don't know what we need to do in order to make progress. We sense that something, some resource, some ability, is missing, but we don't seem to know what it is.

As a matter of fact, we **do** know what's missing, subconsciously. It's our conscious mind that doesn't know. The very fact that we know we need something more shows that we know what it is!

That information can be brought into conscious awareness using the following method (there's an example afterwards):

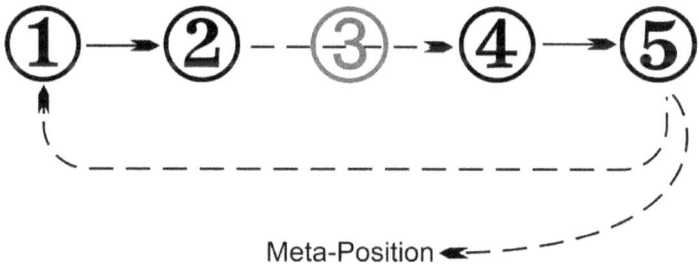

Figure 12: Steps of the Bridge

1. Print out the work materials at the end of this section, cut the page up and place the numbered pieces 1 – 2 paces apart in a straight line, as shown above. The "Meta-Position" piece must be placed to one side.

2. Decide on the problem state in which you find yourself stuck. Go to position 2.

3. Enter the problem state, experiencing it as fully as you're able to. See, hear and feel what it is like to be this way.

4. Allow a movement or body pose that describes this state to you to come up from inside. This may be as simple or as complex as you wish.

5. Break state (spin around, say "banana, banana, banana", sing a silly song, anything you like).

6. Decide on the resourceful state you want to achieve, the way you want to be. Go to position 4, leaving sufficient space for position 3.

7. As before, enter the state and experience it as fully as possible.

8. Allow a movement or body pose that describes *this* state to come up from inside.

9. Move forwards to position 5, which is the end product or outcome of having achieved the resourceful state. It describes how the future will be, once you've gained this resource. Again, allow a movement or pose to appear that describes this state; you'll find that the movement from position 4 to position 5 will be a natural progression from one movement or body position to the other.

10. Break state.

11. Go to position 1, which describes the cause of the problem state in position 2. Get into the feeling of the state. Once again, allow a movement or pose to come up, which describes this state. Moving from position 1 to position 2 will again be performed naturally.

12. Break state.

13. You'll now have two sets of positions:

    • the first pair describes where you are at present, and how you got there (problem state);

    • the second pair describes where you want to go, and how it will change your life (resourceful state).

14. Your task is now to find the bridge between the two sets of states.

15. Go to position 1 and enter the state, taking the appropriate pose or making the proper movement.

16. Move to position 2 and enter its state, progressing naturally from one movement or pose to the other.

17. Keep moving, finding the movement that naturally bridges, at position 3, between positions 2 and 4. Move on to position 5. You should find that traversing from position 1 to position 5 will be one continuous series of movements and poses.

18. Break state.

19. Repeat steps 15 – 18 twice more.

20. Move to the meta-position and consider the movement or

pose at position 3 from an outside view. This movement has a meaning for you. **What is it?** It usually represents a resource you must have, a belief you need to create, a skill you have to develop, or an action you must take, etc., in order to move from the one state to the other.

21. Try on the resource. Act as if you already have it. How would you experience the world differently, if you had and used this resource?

This exercise can be used anytime you cannot see a way of moving from a problem state to a resource state, because it allows your subconscious to communicate without the need for words. Once you have the movement, the meaning is easier to find.

An Example

1. I know that there is something missing in my thinking about teaching.

2. I move to position **2**, sink myself in the feeling, and find a pose that expresses my lack: I hold my hands over my heart, fingers pointing at my chest.

3. Breaking state, I move to position **4**, get the feeling that I have discovered the missing item, and find that the pose is with my hands stretched forwards and upwards, as if reaching to the heavens.

4. Stepping to position **5**, looking to find the feeling of the future I achieve after finding the missing resource, my hands form fists and wave over my head, as if celebrating a huge win.

5. I break state and move to position 1, where the feeling of a total lack of self-esteem leads to a pose with me hugging myself, arms wrapped around me as tightly as possible.

6. I now have two sets of positions:

   • Hands pointing towards heart and hugging myself, representing the problem state and its cause, respectively;

   • Arms reaching upwards, and waving my fists in celebration, representing the desired state and its ultimate outcome.

7. I move to position **1** and take up the pose associated with it. I then move through the positions at a slow walk, changing from pose to pose as I go. I find that there is a pose associated with position **3**. Repeating the steps twice more, the pose is a natural progression from position **2** to position **4**.

8. I step to the side into the meta-position, and consider the pose I found: my hands reach out in front of me on extended arms, palms up, as if reaching for, or out towards, something.

9. Further contemplation reveals to me that the missing resource is dedication to an ideal. I must dedicate myself to teaching something in particular.

10. When I try a feeling of dedication on, a strange thing happens. I must explain that, due to a lazy eye and the results of an eye operation, I have never learned to see three-dimensionally. To me, everything is flat. After I try on the feeling, I notice that people appear to "hover" over the background, as though they were a little closer. This effect has never gone away.

The Bridge: The Movement That Connects

1

2

3

4

5

Meta-Position

Disney Strategy

There are times when the problem is not a hindrance or internal blockage, but instead we need a creative solution to a problem.

This method is based on a technique developed by Walt Disney to create new ideas. He and his ideas team would use three rooms.

1. In the first room, they'd brainstorm new ideas. They weren't allowed to be negative or critical of any ideas, not even their own. The ideas would be written down. When they ran out of ideas, they moved to the next room.
2. In the second room, they'd be critical of how well each idea worked. They were allowed to be negative and destructive of any ideas that had to pass muster. Basically, they decided what it was about the idea that needed to be changed.
3. In the third room, they'd look realistically at each idea, plus the problems they found with it, and work out what adjustments could be made, in order to make the idea workable.

If they weren't satisfied, they'd then go back to the first room and start over.

> *All our dreams can come true if we have the courage to pursue them.*
>
> Walt Disney

Practical Application

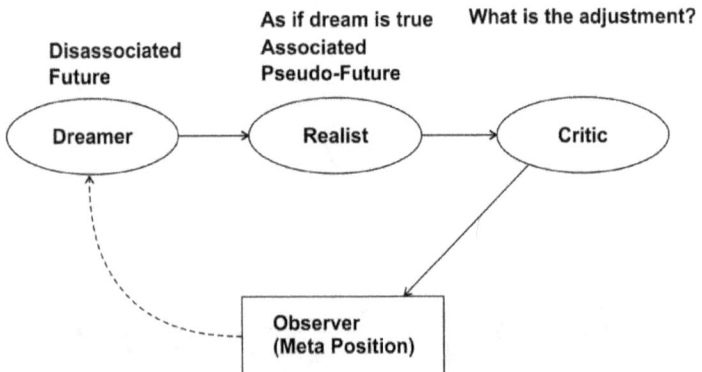

Figure 13: Disney Strategy

1. Print out the page at the end of this section, cut the pieces up, and place them on the floor as shown above.

2. Move to the *Dreamer* position.

3. Find as many creative solutions to your problem as you can, all of them focused on the future, and write them down or otherwise note them. If you're involved in the solutions directly, you must see things disassociated (i.e., you must see yourself in the picture, and not see the picture through your own eyes). You aren't allowed to be negative. Be as crazy and creative as possible. There are no limits.

4. Once you run out of ideas, break state and move to the *Realist* position.

5. Here you must be as realistic as possible about the solutions you created in step 3. Act as if the solutions are true in a "pseudo-future", an imaginary future that may come true. You must be associated and seeing the solutions through your own eyes, as though you were inside the picture yourself. Pretend that you're actually using these ideas. Find all the weaknesses, problems and reasons why not. Tear the ideas apart and discover every possible weakness. Do **not** be self-destructive.

6. Once you've been realistic about every idea, break state and move on to the *Critic* position.

7. Here you must be critical and decide how the solutions must be altered, if necessary, in order to make them workable. Some solutions are beyond redemption. Let them go without regret, because you have an infinity of possibilities available. Other ideas can be saved, but may need to be extended or changed. Some ideas, of course, need no modification at all.

8. Break state and move to the *meta-position*.

9. Consider the ideas you've created, which you've then realistically dissected and judged, with any critical alterations necessary to make them into workable solutions. If you're not satisfied with what you've created, return to the *Dreamer* position, and restart from step 3.

10. If you have one or more useful answers, the exercise is over. Start implementing them!

Incidentally, I've found this method works well with writing books, where the characters become the *Writer*, the *Critic* and the *Editor*!

> *It's kind of fun to do the impossible.*
>
> Walt Disney

Disney Strategy

Dreamer

Critic

Realist

Meta-
Position

Carrying Through to a Successful Dream, and Beyond

> *If a man advances confidently in the direction of his dreams to live the life he has imagined, he will meet with a success unexpected in common hours.*
> Henry David Thoreau

How to Make Your Dreams Real

Now that you have a set of compelling dreams, clear-cut reasons for their achievement, and the emotional fuel to drive them, the process for making them real has already begun. Your RAS will become sensitised as you consistently review your dreams and reasons, and will attract to you any resource of value towards the achievement of your clearly defined desire. Using *Rehearsals* (see page 151) and *Affirmations* (page 161), you'll focus on your goals and dreams.

This continual focus will create neural pathways between where you are now and where you want to go. Because of this intense conditioning, you'll find yourself feeling a sense of absolute certainty that you'll achieve your desires, and this certainty will translate into a quality of action that ensures your success. Your confidence will allow you to attract the appropriate coaches and role models, who'll guide you into taking the most effective actions to produce results quickly.

> *Whatever you do, or dream, begin it now. Boldness has genius, power and magic in it. Begin it now.*
> Johann Wolfgang von Goethe

Reviews

Check your progress regularly, at least once a week at the beginning, to ensure that you're still on the way to where you want to go. In German, there's a maxim that goes "Vertrauen ist gut; Kontrolle ist besser." This translates to "Trust is good; supervision is better." If you start to drift away from the course you set, you can correct it more easily and quickly if you catch it as it starts. The longer you wait, the greater the energy you must expend to get back on course (see *The TOTE Model* in the next section for a more formalised look at the reviewing process). You may even surprise yourself by how quickly you're getting there! This is also a great time to rehearse (see *Rehearsals* on page 151), as well.

If, on the other hand, you discover that the path you're following is not getting you where you want to be, reviews are an ideal place to alter your plans. Simply go back to your list of *Steps to Take* (see page 113) and change the steps, adding, altering or removing as necessary.

When my friends and I started to work on the problems of goal-setting, we tried the traditional method, with an agreement to pair up with someone from the group after six months to review our progress. At that time, we didn't review on a weekly basis, nor did we define outcomes in terms of sensory-specific language; we were setting a baseline for our further investigations.

After six months, I got together with Pat, my partner in this part of the undertaking. I ruefully confessed to doing nothing about any of the goals I'd set myself, with the excuse of being too busy. She told me that we should still check through the list, just to see if I had made any progress, after all.

To my amazement, I'd actually achieved 80% of my goals, without realising it! This goes to show that you have to keep an eye on the progress you are making, to catch the little differences that make a significant difference in the long term. It proves that the myth of the multimillionaire who became so because he didn't know when to stop is no myth at all!

Incidentally, I recently discovered that the 80% figure was typical for most cases where people don't check their progress.

If you find that you've made a mistake or even (horrors!) "failed", remember that there's no failure, only feedback (see page 177). What it's telling you is that you must find another way of achieving your results; this one doesn't work the way you want it to.

> *There is no happiness except in the realization that we have accomplished something.*
>
> Henry Ford

The TOTE Model

The model refers to the basic feedback loop that characterises mental and behavioural strategies (Miller, Galanter & Pribam, *Plans and the Structure of Behaviour*, 1960). The letters TOTE stand for **T**est – **O**perate – **T**est – **E**xit. According to this model, all mental and behavioural programs revolve around a fixed goal and variable means to achieve that goal.

Effective behaviour consists of the following components:

1. A specific goal, clearly represented.

2. A test, sensory or behavioural evidence, to assess whether or not the goal is being achieved.

3. A variable set of means to achieve the goal, to operate to change something or do something to get closer to the goal, if the goal hasn't been achieved.

4. Discern whether the exit criteria are satisfied and exit on to the next step.

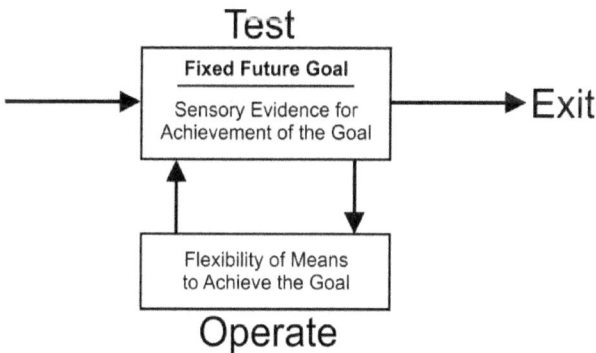

Figure 14: The TOTE Model

What this boils down to is that we look at the direction we're moving in, and compare it with the direction we want to be moving. We make any corrections necessary, and test again. In cybernetics and bionics, this is known as a feedback loop, which is the basis for the control of all actions by living (and other) systems. Thus the process becomes:

T **Test** to see whether we've achieved the goals. If we have, we can exit the loop.

O **Operate** to make progress towards our goal. Usually, we find that either we need to make corrections, or we need continue what we are doing.

T **Test again** to see whether we've now reached our goal.

E **Exit**. We're there!

Our progress tends to look something like this:

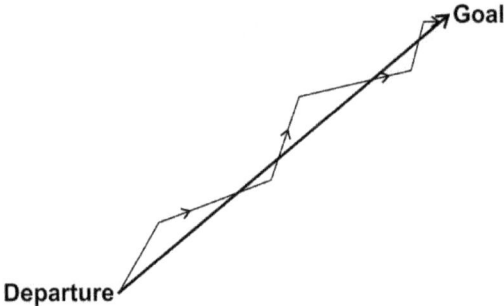

Figure 15: Progress Towards our Goals

This is moving "by and large" towards our goal, a term that derives from manoeuvres necessary to sail against the wind.

Of course, life being what it is, we often find that processes contain other processes, which in turn …

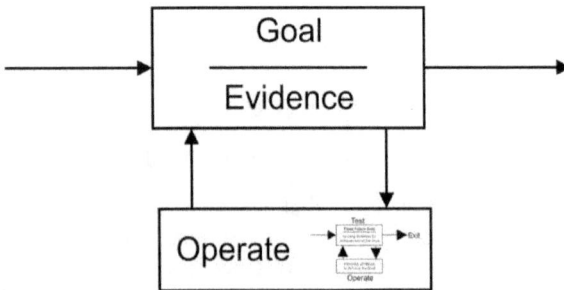

Figure 16: The TOTE Model – Processes Within Processes

At any one time, we may find ourselves dealing with several such self-similar situations, each contained within another. Fortunately, however, the human mind can handle this with ease.

> Great fleas have little fleas upon their backs to bite 'em,
> And little fleas have lesser fleas, and so ad infinitum.
> The great fleas themselves, in turn, have greater fleas to go on;
> While these again have greater still, and greater still, and so on.
>
> Augustus De Morgan, *"A Budget of Paradoxes"*

Applying the TOTE Model to Your Dreams

Read what you wrote down while completing *Creating the Dream* (see page 110) for some of the answers to the questions below.

- What is/are the goal(s) you're working on?

- How do you represent your goals to yourself? As images? Words and sounds? Feelings? A combination?

- What beliefs and values do you have in relationship to your goals?

- What will be your evidence, how will you know you're achieving your goals? What will you see, feel, and/or hear?

- Which sensory modality will you use to evaluate your progress towards your goals? Seeing? Hearing? Feeling? A combination?

- What capabilities and personal resources will you use to achieve your goals?

- How would you like to respond to any difficulties or challenges you may encounter in the process of achieving your goals?

TOTE Model Framework

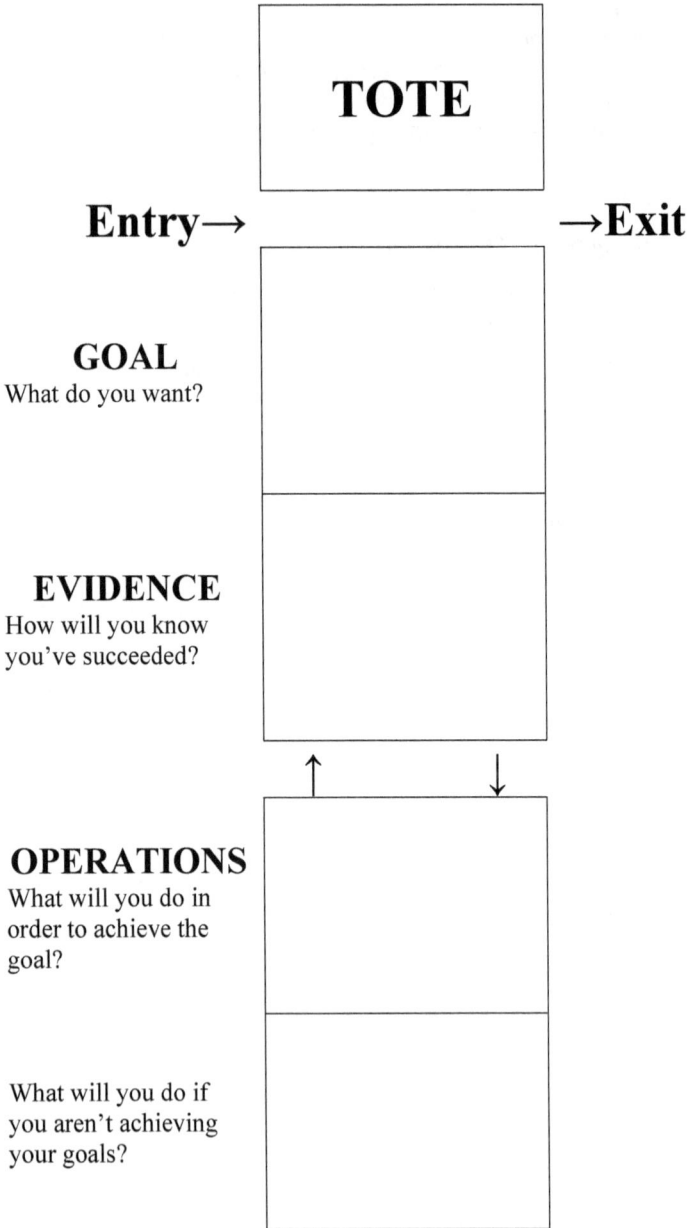

TOTE

Entry→   **→Exit**

GOAL
What do you want?

EVIDENCE
How will you know
you've succeeded?

OPERATIONS
What will you do in
order to achieve the
goal?

What will you do if
you aren't achieving
your goals?

Rehearsals

To ensure the absolute attainment of your dreams, you must condition your nervous system *in advance* to feel the pleasure they'll surely bring. In other words, once or twice a day, you must visualise, rehearse and emotionally enjoy the experience of achieving each one of your most valued dreams. Visualisation (see next section) works because the subconscious mind can't differentiate between external events and internal visualisations. It accepts everything as true. Recalling anything, a dream, thought or memory, reinforces it, making it even more believable for the subconscious. Think positive thoughts and memories for the best effects!

The best times to rehearse are just after you've woken up in the morning, and as you're going to sleep at night. The latter especially so, because you pass the dream on to your subconscious and the universe as you do so. Each time you do this, you create more joy as you see, hear and feel yourself living your dream. It's like rewarding yourself ahead of time! Five minutes for each rehearsal is plenty.

All these positive feelings are related to *Gratitude* (see page 160), and will trigger your RAS and the universe to deliver even more reasons to be grateful.

Visualisation

Visualisation may not be quite what you think it is. Because most people are visual (see *Modalities* on page 46), it's often considered to be picturing things. Indeed, the word itself is a visual word! However, it also includes experiencing what we would hear, feel, etc., creating a holistic (whole) experience.

If we get all the senses involved, the subconscious, which can't discriminate between real experiences and imagined ones, accepts the input as real, and starts working in making it real. The more multisensory input we provide, the more effective it becomes.

Do Something Every Day

While you're rehearsing, why not try the following?

In the morning, after you wake up and do your morning rehearsal, ask yourself what you can **do** during the day to advance towards your goals and dreams. No matter how small, every step will take you that little bit farther.

During the evening rehearsals, ask what you've **done** to get closer to your goals. Reward yourself for every step, making it a part of the rehearsal. That way, you build ever-greater momentum and find yourself rushing towards your dreams.

Keep asking yourself: "What's the next step I can take to achieve my goal?" Listen carefully, because the universe **will** reply to your question with information, intuitions and miracles.

Acts of Faith (Acting "As If")

Acts of faith come in two flavours.

Preparatory

We need to prepare to achieve our dreams, to tell the universe that we're ready. Some possibilities might be:

- If part of your dream is a complete new wardrobe of clothes, get rid of old clothes you no longer wear. You'll be showing that you have space for the new ones. This is also a good idea if you intend to diet. Making space for smaller clothes is a pretty good signal to the universe.

- If you dream of abundance and money, open a new bank account for that money. If you want to invest in stocks and securities, open a trading account at your bank or with a broker.

- How about a relationship? If your life is full of other things, and there's no time or space for a relationship with another person, you're sending a very specific message to the universe. Make the time and space, and the relationship will appear.

Anticipatory

This differs from doing something every day, because it lies closer to *Rehearsals* of your progress (see page 151). In this case, you're practicing how it feels to have already *achieved* your dreams.

For instance, if your dream is abundance, so that you can afford luxuries without having to worry about the costs, you can try some of the following:

- Occasionally buy yourself some small luxury, one that won't break the bank, but is related in some way to the larger luxuries you dream of. Indulge yourself, and get into the feeling of achieving the dream.

- Find out what the costs are of the larger luxuries, enquiring *as if* you're intending to buy, and are simply deciding which company you'll buy from.

- Go window-shopping *as if* you're deciding which colour suits you best.

If you have other dreams, here are some suggestions:

- If you want to be a published author, contact publishers to find out if they publish the type of book you're writing. They might have special requirements for submission, which they'll be happy to tell you. Or you might first contact a literary agent. If you prefer to be an independent author on the Internet, look into the possibilities offered by Amazon, Kindle, CreateSpace, Nook, Kobo, Print on Demand (POD) companies, or even research publishing yourself via a website or on a forum.

- You're looking for a new job or career. Contact companies that are specialists in this new area and arrange for interviews, just to get the practice. Find out how these companies wish to be contacted, and polish your CV to match the format they prefer.

- If one of the dreams is a new car, go to the showroom, sit in the car and imagine that you're about to drive away, having signed all the contracts. Get one of the sales staff to take a picture of you in the car. Take the prospectuses and price lists home, and discuss with the salespeople which options they'd personally prefer.

I'm sure you can think of your own situations.

Remember, acting "as if" means you have to take action!

Milestones and Way Marks

If you look at the list of *Steps to Take* (see page 113) you wrote out earlier (if you did), you'll find that, not only have you broken the way to your goal down into manageable steps, but you've also created a list of milestones and way marks. Each time you tick off one of these, have a small celebration or give yourself a small reward. By rewarding yourself for each successfully achieved step, you encourage yourself to take the next one. This way, you gather momentum and find yourself sweeping on to achieve your goal faster than you thought possible.

PS Don't forget to plan a large celebration for taking the final step and actually **achieving** your dream! Practice celebrating the small successes as a way of rehearsing celebrating the big success. Show *Gratitude* (page 160) that you've accomplished each step.

There's a subtle difference between milestones and way marks, however:

- Milestones are markers to show that you've reached or passed a particular point in your progress. They have an orientation to the past.

- Way marks are the next points you are aiming towards or steering for. Like the way marks in sailing or orienteering, they point towards the future.

Personally, I prefer way marks.

Momentum vs. Inertia

One of the most important things in achieving our dreams is to keep moving! Once we attain a particular momentum, it becomes easier to keep going. In other words, the faster you go, the faster you **can** go. How often have you had to push yourself to start something, and then found that the going got easier once you were moving?

The opposite of momentum is inertia. Doing nothing is the best way to ensure that nothing will happen. There are many who think that sitting at home and visualising their dreams is enough. Unfortunately, it's untrue. You have to work towards your dreams, even if the steps are small ones. Once you start the process, the universe will step in and help you, amplifying your efforts a thousand-fold or more.

> *An object at rest tends to remain at rest unless acted upon by a force. An object in motion tends to remain in motion unless acted upon by a force.*
>
> Newton's First Law of Motion
>
> *The Universe loves speed.*
>
> Dr Joe Vitale

"Being Reasonable"

When we talk about "being reasonable", we must realise that this sentiment is very much a two-edged sword.

On the one hand, if you discover that you're getting nowhere, or you're in a hole and digging yourself in deeper, being reasonable is the sensible thing to do. You look around and decide whether to keep going and modify what you're doing, or if it's time to change direction or even pursue another goal.

On the other hand, many of us use "being reasonable" as a means of limiting our dreams and ourselves. If you only go after "sensible" dreams, you may find yourself achieving them, but you'll also be disappointed and dissatisfied. The secret here is to be as unreasonable as possible, going after dreams that stretch you and take you to heights that you would otherwise never attain.

> *The reasonable man adapts himself to the conditions that surround him...*
> *The unreasonable man adapts surrounding conditions to himself...*
> *All progress depends on the unreasonable man.*
> George Bernard Shaw

Commitment and Persistence

Commitment is the decision to put all your resources into your goal, with no ifs, buts or maybes. For further information, see *There is no abiding success without commitment* on page 203.

> The race is not always to the swift, but to those who keep running.
>
> Anonymous

Persistence, where you keep going, especially when the going gets hard, is absolutely vital to success. "Stick-to-it-iveness" is a prerequisite. If you give up after the first hurdle, I guarantee that you'll never unleash your dreams!

> When everything goes against you, and it seems that you cannot hold on for a minute longer, never give up then, for that is just the time and place that the tide will turn.
>
> Harriet Beecher Stowe

Of course, if you keep going and are **really** getting nowhere, you must remember the difference between persistence on the one hand and obstinacy or obsession on the other!

> The difference between try and triumph is a little umph.
>
> Unknown Author

Gratitude

As you're enjoying the feelings of having achieved your dreams, you can also feel gratitude for having achieved them.

If you feel gratitude for everything you already **do** have, no matter what it is, you'll be increasing your chances of success. In our world, if you've a roof over your head, food to eat, clean water to drink, money and family, you already have more than much of humanity. Be grateful for them!

If you keep thinking gratitude, the Law of Attraction will spring into action, bringing about even more situations for which you can be grateful. In other words, feeling gratitude breeds more chances for feeling gratitude.

If you don't accept whatever's being given and don't feel gratitude, you're pushing it all away. The Universe will take note and remove future opportunities, you ungrateful creature!

Be grateful when someone thanks you or compliments you. Be grateful when they give you something. Don't take their giving away from them. Be especially grateful when the universe gives you something. Money is another form of compliment, so be grateful.

> *If the only prayer you said in your whole life was "thank you", that would suffice.*
>
> Meister Eckhart

Affirmations

Affirmations are written statements of your dreams that you rehearse out loud. For the really dedicated, write them out 20 or more times a day. They can be used to enhance and strengthen your rehearsals (and vice versa). However, they must be something that you can believe in, otherwise all your negative thoughts will arise, going: "Yeah, right!"

If this happens, you need to wear your subconscious down. Persist in your affirmations every day, change the negative thoughts by replacing the negative beliefs behind them (see *Changing Beliefs* on page 173), and eventually you will believe the affirmations.

To be effective, an affirmation must follow certain rules:

1. It must be written in the first person ("I" form). Add your own name for extra effect.

2. It must be written in a positive form, just like an outcome. Include words of emotion, such as "happy," "joyful", etc. for extra oomph.

3. Make sure that it's a single dream / outcome, without contradictions.

4. It must be written in the present tense, as though you've **already** achieved it. Use the word "now" to really hammer this home.

5. It must be specific.

6. As a rider, add the sentences: "This or something better" and "Be it to the highest good of all concerned", for the reasons given in *Creating the Dream* on page 110.

These are very similar to the rules for forming outcomes. In fact, it's a good idea to run any prospective affirmations through the five steps for creating well-formed outcomes (page 89) and the SMART grid (page 102).

Examples of good affirmations:

- I, John, enjoy being a successful entrepreneur

- I, Jane, now manifest a loving relationship in my life

- I, Stephen, am a nurturing and supporting teacher

These are very simple affirmations; you can make yours as complex as you wish. Just remember that, if they're too complicated or have too many different parts, the subconscious could become confused. The keyword here is **KISS**: **K**eep **I**t **S**hort and **S**imple!

Place the affirmation where you see it every day:

- On the refrigerator door.

- On the mirror in the bathroom, where you see it while you brush your teeth.

- Under the computer screen on your desk (be careful here).

- There is now computer software available that will flash it on your computer screen as a subliminal message at random intervals throughout the day, or you could make it part of your screen saver!

Repeat as often as possible.

Emotions

Reread the previous section on *Emotions* on page 109. Once you start using your emotions to create the dreams, continue using them to drive yourself onward to a successful conclusion.

There's a simple formula you can apply that ensures that, by using your emotions, you'll succeed:

Thoughts + Emotions + Actions = Attraction

Taking your thoughts, adding the emotional force of already having achieved them ("Nevillizing" them, Dr Joe Vitale calls it), and taking action to follow through, guarantees that the Law of Attraction will achieve its maximum effect. Using the Law of Attraction requires **action** to work!

When using *Affirmations* (*see previous section*), say them, think them, even write them, with emotional force behind them. Believe in them.

Apropos emotions, there are two that are to be avoided at all costs …

The Two Most Useless Emotions, Ever

There are two emotions that bring nothing but unhappiness into your life. They have no positive side.

Guilt is you saying to yourself: "I've done something wrong in the past, and now I must feel bad about it for the rest of my life."

Really? Why?

If you have done something wrong, is there any way you can make good? Can you apologise to the person(s) you hurt and ask their forgiveness? Can you make restitution another way? If so, why are you still feeling guilty? Just go out and do it.

If not, you must learn to forgive yourself. Forgiveness doesn't mean condoning your behaviour. It means letting go of the guilt, anger, etc. associated with that behaviour and moving on. *Zero Limits* by Dr Joe Vitale and Dr Ihaleakala Hew Len is an excellent place to start.

Either way, learn the lessons from the experience and move on. Scientists have determined that feeling guilty can damage your immune system (see *Psychoneuroimmunology* on page 194).

> *Guilt is the tragic delusion of culpability without the comic relief of sin.*
>
> Thorax
>
> *Sin lies only in hurting other people unnecessarily. All other "sins" are invented nonsense. (Hurting yourself is not sinful – just stupid.)*
>
> Lazarus Long,
> in Robert Heinlein's *"Time Enough for Love"*

Worry is even worse. You're feeling bad about the future, so you worry about it. Here the attitude often seems to be: "I believe something in the future is going to be bad, and I'm going to feel bad about it now, in case it doesn't happen, just to make sure that I don't miss out on all the negative feelings."

That's crazy!

The problem is that people confuse concern and worry. Concern tends to be either neutral or love-based, while worry is definitely fear-based. Being concerned about something or someone means that you don't want something bad to happen. Being worried means that you *dread* something bad happening; you're letting your fear drive you, endlessly and relentlessly obsessing about it. If something bad *has* happened, time enough to feel bad when you do find out about it. Why upset yourself now, when your negative emotions could actually cause the very events you've been dreading to occur (think Law of Attraction)? Even worse, by worrying, you're only increasing your sense of helplessness and powerlessness.

> *You will save yourself a lot of needless worry, if you don't burn your bridges until you come to them.*
> **First Rule of Negative Anticipation**
>
> *I have known a great many troubles, but most of them never happened.*
> **Mark Twain**

In the end, both guilt and worry have the same effects:

- We feel bad about the world and ourselves, which causes us to be stuck where we are, unable to change for the better. The Law of Attraction and our RAS will ensure that we get more of the same, keeping us stuck.

- Our attention is directed away from the present into the past or the future. Either way, we aren't really living. The only time we have is right now. The only existence we have is in the present. Move away from the present, and you have only memory, or anticipation and imagination. Use the present as a gift that is constantly renewed and fresh.

> *If I worry about the future, will the future change?*
> **Quai Chang Caine, in *"Kung Fu"***

The best way to deal with either of these emotions is to do something completely unrelated to them. Pull up weeds, take the dog for a walk, help with the local school sports club, work in a soup kitchen for a few hours, or any action that takes your mind off your guilt / worry. All these things anchor you back in the present and occupy your thoughts with other concerns.

If you ever feel tempted to move away from the present to either the past or the future, remember that it's never the perfect time to do something ... but that change only ever happens **now**.

> *When you live in the past, it costs you the present.*
> **Anonymous**

Dealing with Fear

Fear is a terrible thing to feel, isn't it?

Your hands shake and are sweaty, while your mouth is dry. Your stomach flutters, your breathing is fast and hard, and your heart pounds. You even have bright pictures filling your head about what could happen.

On the other hand, excitement and anticipation are wonderful things to experience:

Your hands tremble, the palms are moist, and you have to wet your lips repeatedly. You have butterflies in your stomach, you breathe quickly and deeply, and your heart races. The brilliant images of your expected outcome buzz in your thoughts.

That's odd! The two sets of symptoms sound pretty much the same, don't they? Where's the difference?

The difference is all a matter of interpretation.

Both are examples of the body preparing to take action. Glands release adrenaline and other useful hormones and chemicals into the bloodstream. Blood is pulled away from nonessential parts of the body. The muscles tense in anticipation of a burst of energetic motion. Biologists call this the "Fight or Flight" reflex. I prefer to think of it as "Action Stations" or "General Quarters".

This was useful for our ancestors, who might need to flee a sabre tooth cat or to attack an invading tribe. They even needed it to chase their meals. These days, this might all seem an overreaction. However, there are still times when we need that burst of energy: avoiding a runaway car, attacking an opposing team member at football, or even running down to the shops because you forgot to buy something for dinner.

So the next time you feel fearful, ask yourself this question: "Is this really fear, or is it, in fact, excitement?" The answer might surprise you. It will certainly help to understand that sometimes our wrong interpretations, and the habits and false beliefs that lie behind them, are the **real** problem.

If you decide that it really is fear, then the next question to ask is "why am I fearful?" Have you overlooked or missed something? Do you need to acquire further information or skills? Is something there that shouldn't be? In every case, fear is a warning that the situation is not all that it seems. It's nothing to be afraid of …!

Carrot and Stick

Some people react better to negative driving emotions. They only go after goals if they're escaping something negative. Rather than chasing the "carrot", they need the "stick" to motivate them. This works, but it's not always an ideal way of doing things, nor is it a very comfortable one. Furthermore, by concentrating on the negative, they're only encouraging the Law of Attraction to give them more of what they've already experienced.

> *You can't punish yourself into change. You can't whip yourself into shape. But you can love yourself into well-being.*
> **Susan Skye**

You must decide for yourself whether you're a "towards" person who follows the carrot, or an "away" person who runs away from the stick. Either way, you can use the necessary emotions to push you the way you want to go.

How about using both options at the same time?

Get two envelopes. One will be used to contain money for a celebration or reward to be given when you've achieved your goal. Put the same amount of money in the other one and address it to an organisation, political party, or any other group you despise; make sure it will be a public donation with your name on it, and that it will be painful for you to make that donation. Hand both envelopes to a friend with instructions to give both of them back to you if you succeed in achieving your goal, or to keep the first and send the second if you don't. Set a reasonable deadline on this, perhaps based on your timeline (*see Setting a Timeline* on page 79). This way, you'll be leveraging both positive and negative emotions to drive you forwards.

Letting Go

One of the most important things we have to learn is to let go. If we keep clinging to our dreams and are not releasing them out into the universe, we're actually preventing the universe from aiding us in achieving them.

Worse, not letting go can be an extreme burden on us, both emotionally and physically. A classic Zen story illustrates this:

Two Zen monks were travelling from one monastery to another. The one was old and experienced, the other young and newly trained. The weather had been bad, so it was no surprise to them to come across a river that had flooded, making the ford across it almost impassable.

Standing crying at the edge of the river was a young geisha, who evidently couldn't cross it. Without saying a word, the older monk tucked his robes up around his thighs, rolled back his sleeves, and picked the girl up. He carried her across the river and set her down on the other side without a word.

The two monks continued their journey in silence, the younger obviously preoccupied with something. When they reached the monastery that evening, he remonstrated with the older monk, telling him that, as monks, they were not allowed to speak with women, let alone touch them. He went on for some time, ending by saying how tired he was.

The older monk looked at the younger with kindness and surprise, and said: "No wonder you are tired. I left the young woman standing by the side of the river. Have you been carrying her all day?"

If you find you're having trouble letting go, remember *Reverse Psychology* on page 66. Write your dream and its description on a piece of paper. Create a little ceremony, burn the paper, and release your dream out into the world, liberating its energy, and handing over responsibility for its achievement to the universe.

Create your dreams, expect them to happen, and then let them go. After all, a trapeze artist can't catch the next trapeze without letting go of the previous one!

Delayed Gratification

Sometimes we don't achieve our goals and dreams because we have cravings. If I'm dieting and suddenly have a craving for ice cream or chocolate, it can throw me completely off stride.

At other times, the problem is fear, even panic attacks, or anger and rage. We can't think straight because our emotions are in the way.

You can deal with both problems using the same little trick: Say to yourself: "OK, I want chocolate", or "I know I want to have a screaming fit", or "I realise that that dress would look really nice, instead of putting the money in the bank."

Acknowledge the emotions and cravings. Then promise them you'll do something when you've finished what you're doing now, or at a particular time. Promises such as "I'll eat some potato chips as soon as I've finished this report for the boss", or "I'll worry about what my partner said about my drinking at precisely 4:30" work.

When you've finished the report, see whether you still want those potato chips or if you feel like worrying when 4:30 rolls around. Funnily enough, very often, the craving or emotion will have passed, and you won't have to yield to them.

You must, however, be prepared to keep your promise, or it won't work in the long run. If you still want that food, or that emotion, or whatever, then indulge yourself and enjoy it without guilt.

Why does this work?

It's very simple, really: your needs, wants and emotions are used to being put off. After all, you've done the same thing to them often enough in the past; in fact, for the whole of your life so far. However, now you're prepared to acknowledge them and give them space, they'll be even more prepared to be put off until a later date. Think of it as a creative way of using a tendency to procrastinate

> *Some years ago, I was working with a friend on a private project. This often entailed working until after midnight, followed by a half-hour drive home. On several occasions, I was so tired that I could hardly keep my eyes open, which isn't a good situation to be in while driving.*

I'd talk to myself, and ask what I would have to do when I arrived home, in order to repay myself for being awake and alert while driving.

The answer would vary: have a whisky and sit down for 5 minutes; make myself a hot chocolate and sit watching cartoons while I drank it; once it was even to get the laundry ready for the next day. It was never the same twice. Whatever it was, I promised to do it, and was prepared to carry that promise out.

Suddenly, I'd be alert and ready for the rest of the drive home. And when I arrived home, I carried out my promise.

I never had an accident due to being overtired!

Breaking the Rules

There will be times when you run up against various "rules" that attempt to block you or reduce your successes. These may be internal beliefs that limit you or external forces from other people and society in general.

Sometimes, limitations can be unconsciously taken over.

A zoo acquired a polar bear from another zoo. Because they'd never owned one before, they had to build a special enclosure for it. This took some months, during which time the bear was kept in a cage. The cage was large enough for the bear to take three steps to the right, and three to the left. The great day came when the bear was released into its new home. Although the enclosure was much larger, for the rest of its life, the bear could only take three steps to the left and three steps to the right.

Young elephants are tied with heavy chains around one leg and steel rods hammered deep into the ground. Try as they might, they can't escape. As they grow older, the chains become lighter. By the time they're adult, light rope and a wooden stake are sufficient to keep them in place. They've come to believe that they can't pull themselves free, and so these simple measures are enough.

What cages and chains have you got in your head that are keeping you from moving towards your dreams?

Take a careful look at these rules, because you may have to break them in order to succeed! They can often be identified by words such as "should", "have to", "ought to" and "must." They often appear with hidden thoughts about what is *really* going to happen (if you're honest with yourself):

- I *should* go and see my sister [but I won't, because I can't stand my brother-in-law].

- You really *ought* to watch that movie [but I know you won't, because you can't be bothered].

- I *must* go on a diet [which I will fall off at the first sniff of a piece of chocolate cake]!

American psychologist Albert Ellis has identified the whole group as examples of "musterbation", because they tell you what you

must do. They are examples of you playing mind games with yourself.

However, they're only rules, not laws. Laws tell us how the universe functions. Rules tell us what we, other people, and society expect from us. Incidentally, man-made laws are really only rules.

If they're your beliefs, and you want to continue towards your goals and dreams, you'll have to change them (*see the next page*). Some of the other exercises in this book will be useful for this, too. NLP and other self-help books will give you other methods to use.

If the rules come from outside, you may have to become a "rule-breaker". There are people who keep rules, and people who break rules. Which are you?

- Would you prefer to learn how to apply the rules even better than you already do, in order to achieve your results?

- Or would you rather break the rules, because you're sure that you know better than other people, what you need to do in order to succeed?

> *There are no rules around here. We're trying to accomplish something.*
> Thomas Edison, remarking about his laboratory
>
> *He that chooses his own path needs no map.*
> Queen Kristina of Sweden

Just remember, the ones who successfully break the rules are the ones who write the **new** rules!

Changing Beliefs

Often we think that negative beliefs are getting in the way, and we must get rid of them in order to succeed. The problem is, sometimes these negative beliefs don't exist at all. However, by concentrating on them and thinking about them, we can create them! In the computer world, the phrase **GIGO** means **G**arbage **I**n, **G**arbage **O**ut. If you put nothing but bad data into your mental computer (e.g., thinking about negative beliefs), you'll get nothing but bad results coming out (i.e., creating those negative beliefs).

Furthermore, if the negative beliefs do exist, by concentrating on them, we're only reinforcing them. The Law of Attraction and the RAS will then ensure that we continue to experience more of the same.

A much better way of dealing with them is to work on the positive beliefs we want to have. By practicing positive beliefs and the actions associated with them, the negative beliefs, if they exist, will slowly weaken and disappear. Behavioural psychologists have used this method successfully for years. If you can't change the belief behind a particular behaviour, you change the behaviour, and **that** modifies the belief. This is an interesting application of the *Logical Levels* (see page 49), using them in reverse, as it were.

The next section, *Presuppositions*, contains a number of positive beliefs you might try. There are many others you can find or create for yourself. Use the method of trying out the presuppositions to change your beliefs. It's really that easy!

Beliefs are often linked with each other in complex ways, forming belief systems. If these belief systems have a negative effect on your life, you should remember that belief system can be abbreviated to BS. And we all know what else BS means ...

Many associate the word "belief" with religion. If this causes problems for you, try using "unconscious programming" instead.

Presuppositions

Presuppositions are assumptions you can make and positive beliefs you can hold. Some of them form part of the basis of NLP. This doesn't mean that they're necessarily **true**, merely that they're **useful**.

> *I'm going to lie to you, but they're **useful** lies.*
> My late friend Dennis, on his NLP courses

I suggest that you try these presuppositions and act *as if* they were true. Play act believing in them, and discover how useful they are for you. Keep thinking about them and how having them changes the way you see the world and how you act. Try them consistently for 21 days before deciding whether to keep them. Experience shows that using something consistently over a period of three weeks gives us enough familiarity to evaluate whether to keep on with it or not.

If you decide to keep a particular presupposition, using it consistently over a period of 60 – 90 days will be enough to ensure that it becomes a habit, and thus a permanent part of your repertoire of strategies. It has become a part of your unconscious competence (see *Learning* on page 41).

You don't need to use them all at once. Just try them out one at a time, and decide which you want to use afterwards. You'll find, however, that they're often entwined with one another.

> *Suck it and see.*
> Old radio advertisement for flavoured boiled sweets

The map is not the territory

People operate from their perspective of the world, rather than what the world really is.

Based on a remark by Alfred Korzybski in his 1933 book *Science and Sanity*, "the map is not the territory" has been defined by Gregory Bateson as one of the underlying concepts behind NLP.

The idea is that, no matter how we conceive the world to be, reality is what it is, and not what we think it is. Each of us has our own map of how we think the world is, but it's no more than a map, as related to reality as an item on a menu is to the actual food being served. On top of that, people respond according to what is in their maps. This explains how two or more people can experience the same event, yet have completely different interpretations of what occurred.

> *A psychology professor in America did a simple test with his students. He showed them a picture of two men standing facing one another; one was white and the other black. The men did nothing but look at one another. The white man stood with his arms folded, an open cutthroat razor in his hand.*
>
> *When asked a month later what the picture had shown, the variation was astounding. Very few could accurately describe the two men at all. The reported actions varied from the men talking to each other to fighting, all the way up to the black man mugging the white one using the razor (and one case even a gun) to threaten him.*

The descriptions said much more about the people giving them than they did about the actual image. The students modified their memories to match their prejudices and expectations, which were parts of their maps of reality.

> We don't see things as **they** are. We see them as **we** are.
>
> Anaïs Nin

How we define character traits is also a function of our internal maps:

> *I'm persistent. You're stubborn. He's pig-headed.*

All three describe the same thing.

This presupposition can be extremely liberating, because it allows us to realise that, no matter how bad things appear to be, it's often only our model of the world that makes everything look bad. If that's the case, we can alter our models and beliefs, and be happier and enjoy the ride. To the universe, it's all the same.

*My assistant at work and I were discussing some changes we had made to a program two months before. I said something about the way the system as a whole worked, and she told me I'd told her something else. She even brought out some notes to show that her point of view was right. She couldn't understand my response: that what she'd written was what she **thought** I'd said, rather than what I'd **actually** said. For her, if it was written down, it was the truth. Her map of reality doesn't contain any other possibilities. To her, what she'd written black on white = reality.*

Moreover, if we change our models, it alters the way we interact with the world, thus allowing us to change reality through our thoughts and actions!

Thousands of years ago, Hindu philosophers were calling this *Maya*, or *The Great Illusion*.

> Humans get so conditioned to looking at the universe in terms of little labelled pieces, they tend to act as though the universe really **were** those pieces. The matrix through which we perceive the universe has to be a direct function of that universe. If we distort the matrix, we don't change the universe, we just change our way of seeing it.
>
> Frank Herbert, *"The Godmakers"*

No matter what, respect the fact that others may have very different maps, and respect the maps that they have. Do this, and you'll find yourself with far fewer conflicts with other people, plus a more tolerant attitude to their foibles (and yours!).

There is no failure, only feedback

This is another liberating presupposition. No matter what you do, you can't fail. You just learn another way of not achieving your result. This is how we learned to crawl and walk. We tried different ways until we found one that worked. If we'd given up the first time we fell down, nobody would walk, or even crawl.

The problem is that many people treat failure as a sentence to death, when it could be one of the most freeing experiences the universe can give us.

The fire brigade was called out one night to deal with the fire at an inventor's laboratory. They couldn't prevent the building from being totally destroyed.

Near the fire stood an elderly man in his nightclothes, with his wife, who was similarly dressed.

"Look, my dear," said the old man to his wife as he held her close, "all our mistakes are going up in smoke!"

The man was Thomas Edison, who still has the American and world records for holding the largest number of patents.

Of course, most of us have heard the story about the young reporter who asked Edison about the fact that he'd had more than 10,000 failures before creating a working light bulb. "No," said the great inventor, "I learned 10,000 ways not to make a light bulb."

If you don't get the results you want, it's a message from the universe that you must change something in the way you're doing things. "If you keep on doing what you've always done, you'll keep on getting what you've always gotten." If what you're doing isn't working, do something else. Treat it as a learning experience.

> A learning experience is one of those things that says, "You know that thing you just did? Don't do that."
> Douglas Adams, "The Salmon of Doubt"

Furthermore, every time we learn something new, we grow and change.

> The only difference between a rut and a grave is in their dimensions.
> Ellen Glasgow

> *One of the worst ways of being stuck and failing is to be a success. That way, we don't try anything new, which might make us even more successful.*
> My late friend Dennis

No matter what happens, you're not a failure!

Mistakes are our friends

This follows on from the previous presupposition.

Mistakes are messages from the universe showing us something we may have missed.

> *Mistakes are a part of being human. Appreciate your mistakes for what they are: precious life lessons that can only be learnt the hard way. Unless it's a fatal mistake, which, at least, others can learn from.*
> Al Franken

Think of Fleming finding a contamination in his experiments, which led to the discovery of penicillin. How about the employee of 3M who didn't apply glue to the whole surface of a piece of paper, giving the world Post-It®?

Instead of thinking of events as mistakes, start thinking in terms of happenstance, serendipity or "happy accidents" (television painting teacher Bob Ross). It won't stop "mistakes" from happening, but you'll look at them with a different eye, seeing them as possible shortcuts or even gifts from the universe, giving you something you might never have conceived of on your own.

> *The reason I know so much is because I have made so many mistakes.*
> Richard Buckminster Fuller, in *"Critical Path"*

All our life experiences are encoded in our neurology

This is another way of saying that we remember everything that has ever happened to us, even if we can't recall it. The experiences are all there, to be used when necessary.

They're stored in our brains and bodies. Recent research shows that, throughout the body, the molecules of memory and emotion called neuropeptides are present in all our nerve cells, not just those of the brain, as had been previously thought. Further research also indicates that the individual internal organs themselves produce these same chemicals. Literally, our bodies remember and think for themselves. Methodologies such as John Veltheim's *Body Talk* are based on this concept.

Proof for this comes from transplant technology. There have been cases of transplant organ recipients showing changes after the organs started to integrate into their bodies:

- Lifelong vegetarians have suddenly developed cravings for meat, and vice versa.

- Classical music buffs started attending and enjoying heavy metal concerts.

- People have had memories of events that never happened to them.

- New behaviour patterns and habits have manifest themselves from nowhere.

All of these were patterns in the lives of the donors that transferred themselves to the recipients.

The downside to all this can be that all our beliefs are also part of our experience and therefore part of our bodies and nervous systems. They affect how we see the world (see *The map is not the territory* on page 175).

Individuals process all information through their five senses

Everything we experience is processed by our senses: sight, hearing, touch, taste and smell. No matter what happens, these are the gateways we use to understand the world (see *Modalities* on page 46).

All our senses are working all the time, even when we're not aware of the input consciously. To check this out, answer the following question: which foot is warmer, the left or the right? Whichever it is, you weren't consciously aware of the difference until I asked the question. However, the input was being fed into your brain, and stored with all the other input in your subconscious.

And before somebody else brings up intuition or the sixth sense, I want to say that even here, the main five senses play their part. Every extrasensory experience is interpreted through one or more of them: a "flash" of insight (visual), a "still, small voice" (auditory), a "gut feeling" or a hunch (kinaesthetic), etc.

Subjective experience is composed of images, sounds, feelings, tastes and smells

This presupposition follows on from the previous two.

It's true on two different levels:

1. There are times when we ignore the sensations coming in from the outside world, and concentrate one or more of our senses in our inner world. This could be triggered by as simple an experience as smelling a particular smell (e.g. fresh-baked bread), and suddenly seeing a mental image of your grandmother's house, where she was always baking. For a moment, the outside world no longer existed to your sight. Thus, we're always using all our senses, either internally or externally.

   This explains the effectiveness of *Visualisation* (see page 152), because the subconscious mind can't tell the difference between real (external) events and imagined (internal) events. They're all accepted as equally real.

2. On another level, *all* experiences are subjective. Nothing that we experience is unaffected by what's gone before. Our previous experiences, beliefs, models of reality and even our physiological state affect how we interpret what we sense.

   Thus, even the most "objective" experience is actually subjective, because it has to pass through our filters and beliefs, which we use to program the RAS. If you hear children screaming when you're depressed, you have a different interpretation of the sound than when you're feeling upbeat. In the one case, they sound angry or in pain. In the other, they're simply screaming with joy as they play.

Every behaviour serves a positive intention

All behaviour is or was adaptive in the original context (i.e., it was created to deal with a new situation). However, once established, behaviours tend to linger on. No matter how negative a particular behaviour may seem, the intention of the person to whom the behaviour belongs is, or was, positive when it was first established. The problem is that the positive intention may no longer be within reach of the conscious mind.

> *When I was training in NLP in Bali in 1993, one of the teachers was called Jan. He worked with the police and prison authorities of his country of residence in reducing recidivism[2] among prison inmates.*
>
> *He told us about a cat burglar who had been remanded in prison. Jan worked together with him to discover what his positive intentions were. It turned out that he was unemployed, couldn't find any work, and was trying to put food on the table for his wife and children. Adding to that the fact that it gave him a certain thrill to break into houses, and he had plenty of reasons for going back to a life of crime when he left prison.*
>
> *After the man was released, Jan helped him to get into a career as a free-fall parachute instructor. The man now has a successful business, providing for his family, and getting his thrills from the jumps. He finds he has no need or wish to burgle anymore.*

Furthermore, the secondary gain (see point 5 in *Motivation: Reasons for Aiming for this Goal or Dream* on page 107) may also be getting in the way; it's the positive intention in a disguised form.

---

[2] A legal term meaning "habitual relapse into crime".

People make the best choices they can at the time

Any behaviour represents the best choice available at that moment.

Sometimes the choices we have are in a very limited range. It's not because other choices are unavailable. We're simply unable to make or even see them, because of circumstances, life history, resources, beliefs and values at the present time.

*Another case that Jan told us about was a hen-pecked husband who murdered his wife. It turned out that she'd put him down so much that he feared that his personality would collapse into nothing! The years of nagging and suppression had left him unable to see any other choice than destroying the cause of his pain. But there was a positive intention (*see the presupposition above*) to his behaviour: he was able to retain his personality.*

Individuals have all the resources necessary to make any desired change

Each of us has the resources we need to achieve what we want. We create our own reality. If you think you don't have a particular resource (a skill or a particular piece of information), you can find it, because every resource is either already inside you, or it's out there, somewhere. However, "external" resources are simply a reflection of internal resources, in that external reality is a reflection of our internal reality (state).

You might be surprised at the resources you have inside yourself. After all, you've already spent a lifetime learning new things and ideas. All you need is a way to find them. How about using *The Bridge* (see page 135) to search for them?

You can also employ methods you use to solve other problems, even ones that, at first glance, are completely unrelated to what you're doing right now. For instance, it was the study of fluid dynamics (how liquids flow from place to place) that led to better designs for emergency exits. The problem of why megawaves (waves 100 and more feet high) suddenly appear out of nowhere in the middle of the ocean was finally solved using Schrödinger's wave equation, a fundamental equation of Quantum Theory.

> *Destruction: "Then she [Death] told me that everyone can know everything Destiny knows. And **more** than that. She said we all not only **could** know everything. We **do**. We just tell ourselves we don't to make it all bearable."*
> *Dream: "I find that unlikely."*
> *Delirium: "She is right. Kind of. Not knowing everything is all that makes it okay, sometimes."*
> Neil Gaiman, *"The Sandman: Brief Lives"*

If you're really sure that a resource isn't inside you, look outside. Get a mentor or coach, surf the Internet, buy books on the subject, ask someone who already does what you want to learn, outsource what needs to be done; there must be thousands of ways of discovering it.

If you think you can't find what you need, either inside yourself or outside, you need to ask yourself: "Why am I stopping myself from getting any further?"

The resources you need **are** available!

People are your greatest resource

No matter what modern business practice says, **people** are the greatest resource you have. They can:

- teach you how to do things you never did before,
- do things for you that you may not have the time or the ability to do (outsourcing),
- encourage you,
- help you,
- be mentors and teachers,
- even be a source of income, if you act as a resource for them!

Of course, **you** are the greatest resource of them all!

Mind and body are part of the same cybernetic system

There is no thought you can have that doesn't affect your body. Conversely, there is no sensation anywhere in your body that doesn't cause a thought, even if it's on the unconscious level. They directly influence one another. The connection is so strong that the phrases "a unit of mind" and the "bodymind" have been coined to express the fact that they are the same system. This presupposition is the basis of holistic medicine.

Try the following experiment. If possible, have someone read it to you while you listen with closed eyes. Imagine the following:

You're walking in the door of your home. As you look around, you decide to go into the living room. You see your favourite chair, the one you usually sit in. Go and sit down and feel the chair. Look around. You can see everything there: a TV, if you have one, maybe some books or magazines, a table. Take a deep breath and smell the scents you know so well. This room is very familiar to you.

Now get up and go into your bedroom. There is the bed you spend ⅓ of your life in. Lie down for a moment. Relax and think about how you're going to enjoy going to sleep tonight.

Now get up and go into the kitchen. You can see the sink, the cooker, and the cupboards. On one side, you notice a large bowl of fruit. You admire the different colours of the fruit in the bowl: greens, reds and oranges. On top of all the other fruit, you see a lemon. You pick it up, note the yellow colour, and feel the waxiness of the skin. A knife is lying next to the bowl. Pick the knife up and cut the lemon in two. You notice that the flesh is a paler colour than the skin. Lifting the lemon to your mouth, you take a bite and feel the saliva running in your mouth.

Where's the lemon?

I've just created a physical reaction in you, without being anywhere near you, using my words and your thoughts, and without anything physical actually occurring, except for the saliva at the end.

How about another example?

Think about how someone who's feeling depressed sits. I don't mean someone suffering from depression, but we all feel "down" from time to time.

Sit that way, and see how it feels. Your shoulders are slumped, your head down, and your eyes are looking at the floor. Your arms hang at your side or are folded in your lap. Your face is probably slack, frowning, or with some similar expression. This isn't a very nice feeling, is it?

Now! Straighten your back, throw your shoulders back and open your arms wide. Look slightly upwards. Take a deep breath and **smile**.

Now try to feel depressed in this position!

It's very difficult, if not impossible, to feel "down" when your body is in a position saying "up."

Again, I've created a reaction in you without actually being there. In this case, I caused an emotional change just by altering the state of your body.

So, by being careful what you think and what you do with your body, life can be changed in the blink of an eye.

If it's possible for someone, it's possible for me

This can also be stated as follows: *We all have the same neurological systems.*

A moment's thought will prove this true. After all, if everyone has a different nervous system from everyone else, there's no way we could communicate with one another. We wouldn't be able to understand each other's emotions or thoughts. The experiences encoded in your nervous system are different from those of every other person alive, of course. The process of encoding them and using them is the same for each of us.

> *You are unique; just like everyone else.*
> Anonymous

It helps us get over the fear of failure (see *There is no failure, only feedback* on page 177), as well as helping us break through the barrier of our beliefs in our limits. What we think are our limits fall far short of our true limits.

It's also an excellent way of dealing with the feelings of being overawed by others; they're basically the same as you are, feeling the same feelings and having pretty much the same thoughts. Understanding any differences in how they think can be a useful way of learning (*see the section on modelling on the next page*).

This means, if I study how you do something, and learn how to get myself into a similar physiological, neurological, psychological and emotional state as you, I can do the same things that you can. It doesn't necessarily mean that I'll ever be as good as you, although with time I might actually outdo you, because anything is possible. It does mean that I can vastly improve how I do those things. I doubt I shall ever be able to run as well as Usain Bolt or Moh Farra, but if I study them long enough and intensively enough, and practice the same way they do, I'll be able to improve my own running style.

It also explains why nobody broke the four-minute mile until Roger Bannister finally did; nobody believed it was possible. Within a year, several others beat his record. They suddenly realised that it was possible.

> *It always seems impossible until it's done.*
> Nelson Mandela

This presupposition is the basis of modelling the behaviours of others, as well as that of establishing rapport with them.

Modelling successful behaviour leads to excellence

Think about this: everything we learn as babies, we learn by modelling the behaviour of our parents or other carers, older siblings, and others in our environment. We copy the way they eat, walk, talk, everything. Our brains and bodies are designed to learn from other people, and we never really lose that ability. However, we do it unconsciously.

Modelling is doing this consciously, acting "as if" we already had the abilities and capabilities we seek (see *Learning* on page 41 for more information).

As an example of modelling, an experiment by the US Army shows how effective it can be. Two groups of people being trained to shoot pistols were used in the experiment.

Normally, when soldiers are being trained to use the Colt .45 Pistol, there's a success rate of less than 50%, and the trainees use around 2,500 rounds of ammunition per group. This is, among other reasons, because they are told from the beginning that more than half of them will fail, since shooting is so difficult to get right. This was the control group.

The second group was told that firing the pistol was a natural and easy thing to do, because it used skills that they already had, but in a new combination that they hadn't yet learned. They would be successful, they were told. Furthermore, they were taught to model the shooting practices of successful marksmen and women, such as relaxation before firing, etc.

When the results were analysed, the control group showed the expected results: less than half passed the course, and they used a lot of bullets. The second group all passed the course. Indeed, most of them received their marksman's medals, because they were so good. And they used little more than 1,000 bullets to get that result.

So, learn to model the best, and you can become one of the best!

I am responsible for what happens to me

Admit it, you've played the *Blame Game* at one time or another: it's your partner's fault, your boss's, your secretary's, the guy who cut you up on the road, "Them", "The Powers That Be", etc., etc., et-bloody-cetera. Or perhaps you prefer to be a victim and play *Poor Me*.

Either way, no matter what happens, it's not your fault, is it?

Sorry to disappoint you, but that's not true!

Of course, it's easier to blame others for what happens, because then you don't have to do anything about the situation. You don't have to put things right yourself. But remember, by blaming others, you are handing over your power to them. **They** decide whether you feel happy or not. This is the way to become a vict*im* and not a vict*or*.

However, being responsible is not the same as blaming you for what happens!

It means that, at some conscious or unconscious level, you've attracted, invited in, or even caused the events of your life to happen to you. All beliefs, issues and concerns in life, whether conscious or unconscious, have an effect on what happens to you, with the unconscious having the advantage in any conflict of interests.

In other words, one of the following three situations may be true:

1. You cause the events. Something inside you, either conscious or unconscious, is the cause of the events. Beliefs about the world can trigger events that prove their truth, at least as far as you're concerned.

2. You are complicit. Someone or something else is the original cause of the events, but at some level, you conspire with them so that the events happen to you. This is often a confirmation of some strongly held belief within you (e.g., "all men are bastards", or "everyone is out to get me").

3. You allow the events to happen. For instance, if you believe that you aren't worthy, you may let someone swindle you, or otherwise cause you pain. This is the path of passivity.

However, there are caveats:

- You might be attracting these situations into your life

because they have something to teach you. Many believers in Karma and reincarnation consider this to be true.

- There is such a thing as being in the wrong place at the wrong time. The flow of life in our current culture simply put you in the path of events, to your detriment. But do ask yourself why you were in that place at that time.

Even if you aren't responsible for the cause, you **are** responsible for how you react to what happens. Your emotional responses, and what you do about a situation, are all under your control and are your choices to make. It all depends on your focus (see *People choose what they want to focus on* and *How we focus changes how we remember*, both on page 37).

Sometimes, responsibility can be written as response-ability, meaning that we all have the ability to respond to situations. What you decide to do is the most important thing in that situation. Do you panic or freeze up? Do you moan about how everything always happens to you? How about rolling up your sleeves and getting down to doing something about it? Whatever the response, it's **your** decision and therefore **your** responsibility. You're responsible for your **re-**actions as well as your **actions**! As am I for mine.

Once you start to use this presupposition, you realise just how strongly the Law of Attraction has affected, is affecting, and will always affect your life.

To illustrate, here are two examples I came across:

The convalescent airman

At a disco on a NATO base in Germany, I met a young airman who was celebrating his return to Britain in a few days' time. He was in the military fire brigade and had been stationed in Germany for three years. Strangely enough, he'd actually worked for less than three months during those three years.

It seems that he'd been involved in a prolonged series of motoring and work-related accidents, such as: being hit by a driver who ran a red light, being rear-ended by a large truck, or being the middle driver in a multiple pileup, etc. The strange thing was, it was never his fault. He was always the victim (really, this time!). Moreover, he'd never been involved in an accident before arriving in Germany. Each time, he spent weeks in hospital for broken bones and other injuries, followed by convalescence with physical rehabilitation. He showed me an amazing collection of scars.

However, while talking further with him, I discovered something very interesting: he hated Germany and Germans. I never found out why. Unfortunately for him, the fire brigade is the only part of the military that's kept up to full strength, even if it means employing local personnel. This meant that he had to work closely with Germans, which he hated doing.

Here's what I believe really happened:

The first accident may have been exactly that, an accident. However, while he was in a military hospital and during convalescence afterwards, his subconscious learned a crucial lesson: during this time, he didn't have to work with Germans! After that, his subconscious attracted one accident after another, as a way of staying away from Germans. A very painful way of resolving the issue, but one that worked very well indeed!

Rats!

While I was in Bali taking part in my first NLP seminar, I stayed with the rest of the group in a hotel that was directly next to rice fields. As a result, we were very "close to nature".

It was a common experience to hear tree rats running under the eaves or to find a gecko clinging to the wall just under the ceiling. The local inhabitants even caught a snake or two. Having lived in the Mediterranean area for several years, I have no problems with this situation. After all, in one house in Cyprus, the tree rats used to run races under the eaves during the night, from one end of the house to the other and back again.

However, in the room next to mine was a young American woman who hadn't been "hardened" the way I had. Basically, she had a rabid fear of mice, rats, and similar creatures.

Guess who had tree rats paying personal visits every

night? (Hint: it wasn't me!) It got so bad that she had the hotel staff place traps around her room, which were full every morning, with no end of new rats in sight. Eventually, she moved out altogether and went to another hotel.

As another participant of the course remarked: "If you don't resolve your issues inside yourself, the universe will keep presenting you with opportunities to deal with them outside yourself."

And that was exactly the problem: she was so afraid of rats that she attracted them to her. Fear is an attracting emotion, like love and hate. It brings precisely what's feared into our lives, until we learn how to deal with it. We must let go of our fears, and become neutral, before they leave us alone.

I haven't used any examples from my own life because it's easier to see the causes in the lives of others than in your own.

Psychoneuroimmunology

If you're thinking that this is little more than New Age psychobabble, consider psychoneuroimmunology, an area of medical research that examines possible psychological and psychosomatic causes for diseases and illnesses.

The results are fascinating.

According to the scientists involved, at least 95% of all illnesses and diseases have a psychological element as their cause. This explains two apparently contradictory observations:

1. Stress can cause illnesses. This is well a well-known phenomenon, resulting in the loss of billions in income every year, not to mention the distress it causes the victims. The immune system can't cope with both the assault of stress and the attack of the invading bacteria and viruses.

2. The person who collapses into illness *after* a crisis is over and the stress reduced. The person was often already sick, but "couldn't afford to take the time off". Their immune system and bodies kept going until they could afford to relax. They could then "acknowledge" the illness and take the necessary time off. Those who can never let go can literally die on the job.

I've come across a number of interesting cases over the years:

A man had been diagnosed with cancer and was terminal. His doctor, who was also a registered medical researcher, was able to obtain an experimental drug with which to treat him. After a series of injections, the man was found to be cancer free. When rumours started that this particular drug wasn't in fact the magic bullet that everyone had thought, the man's cancer returned. The doctor realised what had happened, persuaded the man that he had a new version of the drug, and injected him with a placebo. The cancer went away again. When the final reports came out that the drug was totally ineffective, the man was dead within six weeks of reading the news. He died of cancer.

There have also been cases of mothers diagnosed with terminal cancer who wished to see their children graduate from university or marry. They fought off the disease for decades, only to succumb within weeks or even days of attending the graduation or wedding.

In another case, a woman was in the psychiatric ward of a prison because she suffered from multiple personality disorder. One of her personalities had murdered her husband. The "wife" personality was a typical dowdy, downtrodden housewife. The "murderer" personality was definitely very sexy, beautiful and independent. What's of interest to us here is the fact that the wife personality was a diabetic, with all the modifications of blood chemistry that that implies, while the murderer personality wasn't. The changes back and forth in the blood chemistry were noticeable within an hour of the change from one personality to the other.

When I was in Bali, a young woman on the course was cured of chronic hay fever by purely psychological techniques. She was actually able to sniff flowers for the first time in her life without having a violent sneezing fit!

An interesting side effect of this research was the discovery that *100%* of accidents have a psychological cause (remember the young airman?). Talk about responsibility!

Everything happens for a reason and a purpose, and it serves us

This relates to the previous presupposition. If we attract bad things into our lives, they're telling us something about our selves, our beliefs, our values and ourselves.

A good question to ask yourself is: "Why is this happening to me?" but with the proviso that you look inside yourself and answer it honestly.

Don't say: "It's my fault because I'm a bad person" or something similar. That's a cop-out. The reason is more likely to be that you have subconscious feelings of low self-esteem or *guilt* (see *The Two Most Useless Emotions, Ever* on page 164), or negative beliefs that are causing the attraction. Whatever it is, you can do something about it.

A good place to start is if you find yourself with health problems and/or chronic illnesses. Talk to yourself, and ask your problem or illness why they are manifesting. Act as if the illness or problem is another person with whom you can discuss things.

> *For a long time, I was exhausted all the time, and kept suffering from upset stomachs, arthritic pains in the knees, insomnia, and other problems. It was only when I talked to myself in the shower one morning, and asked myself what the problem was, that I got an answer. I was "sick and tired" of the job I was in, and this was literally manifesting itself in my health, a phenomenon known as "organ talk" (see* Psychoneuroimmunology *in the previous section).*

Read Shad Helmstetter's book *What to Say When You Talk to Your Self* to learn more about communicating with yourself.

On the other hand, this can also be positive!

> *When I decided to train as a Reiki Master, the question came up: how was I going to pay the tuition fee, which was $10,000 spread over two payments, one at the beginning and one before completion. As the time for the first payment approached, I became a little worried, but decided to let the universe provide. An unexpected bonus at work converted to exactly $5,000, which was what I needed. The payment at the end appeared in a similar way (I was "forced" to have my copious overtime paid out instead of taking time off).*

Of course, this was all "serendipity" or "good luck", wasn't it? For me, it was proof that the universe wanted me to become a Reiki Master!

> Coincidence is how God remains anonymous.
>
> Anonymous

Attitude is more important than aptitude

> *The trick is in what one emphasizes. We either make ourselves miserable, or we make ourselves happy. The amount of work is the same.*
>
> Carlos Castaneda

Are you a "can do" or a "can't do" person? "Gung ho" or "gone home"? "Whatever it takes" as opposed to "whatever"? No matter what your attitude, it's going to determine in large part how successful you are in realising your dreams.

> *Just do it!*
>
> Nike advertising slogan

The unsung genius is a cliché, but still true. Sitting around talking about what you're going to do won't help you achieve it. Neither is just visualising how great the future is going to be, without going and doing something about it.

> *I hear and I forget. I see and I remember. I do and I understand.*
>
> Kung Fu Tze (Confucius)

If you're playing *Poor Me*, then the universe is going to accept the typecasting, and will give you plenty of chances to play the role.

> *If you say that you can or you say that you can't, you're right.*
>
> Henry Ford

It isn't how good we are, but how **think** we are and how we use what we have, that's important.

> *Do what you can, with what you have, where you are.*
>
> Mike Dooley

Individuals with the most flexibility have the highest probability of achieving the response(s) they desire

This means being adaptable, **not** giving way to others. The more flexible you are, the more possibilities you have for achieving what you want. The higher the flexibility, the greater the number of options you can see. The greater the number of options, the more likely you are to succeed in getting your way.

It's as simple as that.

> *Insanity: doing the same thing over and over again and expecting different results.*
>
> Albert Einstein

It's not necessary to understand everything to be able to use everything

When I was young, I was an absolute terror! I had to know how everything worked, so I took things apart. The only problem was, I couldn't always get them put back together properly ...

Now I'm older, I realise that you don't have to know how it works, although that can be interesting. All you really need to know is how to *use* it, whatever it is. I don't know, and will probably never know, exactly how my car works, although I have a general idea. This doesn't stop me from driving.

I'm a Reiki Master, but I've no idea how the initiation ritual works, neither do I know how Reiki itself works. I just know how to initiate and how to use Reiki. It's the same with everything else in life, if you think about it.

I've absolutely no idea *how* the Law of Attraction works, either, even when I see its effects in my life.

I don't need to.

Neither do you.

Work is play

Have you ever done something you enjoyed so much that you wanted to repeat it again and again? What if that was your work?

You can go about this in two ways:

1. Change your attitude to your work. This may be easier than you think. If you look at what you do at work, I'm sure you'll find parts that are fun for you. Use these as rewards for finishing those parts that aren't so enjoyable.

2. Discover what you *really* want to do in your life, and go out and do it. Did you know that in the Western world, the average person pursues around 3½ different careers during their working lives? Maybe all you need to do is make that change? Who knows?

   You do!

> Do what you love and you will never work again a day in your life.
>
> Kung Fu Tze (Confucius)

There is no abiding success without commitment

> *When it comes to a meal of eggs and bacon, the chicken is involved, but the pig is committed.*
> **Anonymous**

Commitment is the will and the drive to succeed, no matter what (see *Commitment and Persistence* on page 159). If you're committed to doing something, using all your skills and abilities, nothing, but nothing, will stop you. Commitment is a statement of faith in yourself, in effect saying:

> *"I believe that I can do it, and that I'm worthy of achieving it. There's nothing in the world that will stop me from getting there."*

Also, stop using the word "try". That word gives you permission to fail, whilst making a great deal of noise. Work at ensuring that you've zero alternatives, no other possibility but success. As they say: "Failure is not an option". Variations on "try" like "attempt", "have a go" and "take a whack at" are also on the blacklist.

> *There is do and do not. There is no "try".*
> **Jedi Master Yoda, *"The Empire Strikes Back"***

All learning experiences are growth experiences

Every time we learn something new, one of two things can happen:

1. The fact fits in with what we already know. In this case, the experience extends our knowledge, and we grow.

2. There is a *cognitive conflict*, where either the facts contradict what we already "know" to be true, or we have no framework available at all in which to insert them. If this happens, we can react in various ways:

   a. If there's a contradiction, we can restructure the knowledge we have in order to accommodate the new information. The more fundamental to a structure the facts are, the more radical changes become. Also, the older we get, the larger the structures become, and the harder it is to make the changes. However, it can be done. I've seen 60-year olds learning to use a computer with ease! And so we grow.

      During the restructuring, we may find that we become confused, because the old information is no longer available in the usual form, and the new information isn't yet completely in place. Just remember: confusion is good because it shows that you're learning something new. However, many use this as an excuse to go back to the old ways moving to option **b**.

   b. We ignore the new facts. Many fundamentalists choose this option as a matter of course, because they can't or won't change something they perceive as part of the basis of their very being. They reject the learning experience out of hand and don't grow.

   c. Some adopt a third strategy, which I call "pseudo-growth". They hold the facts, isolated from the rest of their knowledge structures, ready to trot them out to prove that they've learnt them. The facts are encysted and have no real effect on them. They don't grow either, because they too haven't truly learned.

> *When you're finished changing, you're finished.*
> Benjamin Franklin

All growth is risk-taking

Some people around you may not react positively to your growth and change. These naysayers usually say something like:

"We like you just the way you are!"

> Be who you are and say what you feel, because those who mind don't matter and those who matter don't mind.
>
> **Dr Seuss**

The reason for this is very simple: if **you** change, then **they** have to change, too. Most people are incredibly resistant to change.

> Faced with the choice between changing one's mind and proving there is no need to do so, almost everybody gets busy on the proof.
>
> **Galbraith's Law of Human Nature**

Of course, the only person you have the right to change is yourself. If you want to change the behaviour of others, you must first change your own behaviour.

> **Be** the change you wish to see in the world.
>
> **Mahatma Gandhi**

Just the same, there is a risk factor, and you must be prepared to take that risk if you want to grow. I have lost friends who didn't want to change, and so wandered out of my life when I did. One of them did so quite violently, accusing me of theft and all sorts of other crimes, none of which were true. I still have no idea what the trigger was. Perhaps he was just unable to let our friendship go, and so had to find a plausible reason (in his mind) for dropping me.

> The person who says it cannot be done should not interrupt the person doing it.
>
> **Chinese Proverb**

The universe we live in is friendly and abundant

If you believe in scarcity, then scarcity is all that you'll experience. If you believe in abundance, you'll have abundance. And if there's abundance, then you'll be happy when others find abundance too because you know that having something doesn't mean that others are being deprived, or vice versa. We all want different things.

Even worse, if you believe that the world is a dangerous and hostile place, you'll live in fear because the universe will show you a dangerous and hostile face. If the world is friendly, you'll find friendliness all around you and you'll be friendly. Have you ever noticed that many of the people who believe that the world is hostile are themselves hostile to the world?

> *If you dream that everyone might be your enemy, one day they may become just that.*
>
> Nick Cohen

Socrates sat on a rock outside the gates of Athens, watching people entering and leaving the city. He saw a man with a grim expression on his face approaching, carrying a pack of belongings. He stopped the man and asked him where he was going.

"I am coming to Athens to live," said the man.

"And what sort of town have you come from?" enquired Socrates.

"A terrible place," lamented the man. "It is full of people with bad manners and terrible behaviour, nothing but liars, thieves, murderers and prostitutes."

"Then I suggest that you seek elsewhere," advised Socrates, "for you will find nothing more than the same if you come here to live."

The man grumbled to himself, then continued down the road.

A short while later, another encumbered man was walking towards the city gates. He had a smile on his face. Socrates stopped him and asked him where he was going.

"I am travelling to Athens to seek a new abode," said the man.

"And where have you been living? What sort of town is it?"

"It is a wonderful place," boasted the man, *"full of pleasant and friendly people who are always ready to help their neighbours, with loving hearts and kind faces."*

"Stay here and be welcome, then," said Socrates, *"for you only find more of the same kind of people."*

> *He who fears something gives it power over him.*
> Arab proverb

Either way, the universe doesn't care what you think, but it **will** reflect back what you think about it!

What do **you** believe about the universe?

Points to Remember

- Our dreams affect us, whatever they may be.

- The thoughts we habitually project (think) affect us **enormously**, whatever they are.

- Therefore, you shape your own existence with the thoughts you choose to consistently project every moment of your life.

- It isn't achieving a dream that matters, so much as the quality of life you experience along the way, every day. It's who you come to be during the journey that's important. You have to **become** a person worthy of achieving that goal or dream.

- Whether your dreams materialise instantly, or take shape gradually over time, the only limit to what you can have in your life is the size of your imagination and the level of your commitment.

- All dream creation must be followed by both:

  o The development of a plan or plans

  o Persistent action towards carrying out the plan.

- Train yourself to focus on improvements, no matter how small. In NLP, this is referred to as "the difference that makes a difference".

- As you approach the achievement of your dream, start thinking about moving the goalposts, i.e., creating new dreams. This is very important, because otherwise you might start sabotaging your own efforts. And think about what happens if you don't have a new goal. For example:

  o The person who looks forward to retiring, without any idea of what to do once they are retired, often has a very short life expectancy after retirement!

  o Once someone has become a star (pop, film, etc.), if they have no goals afterwards, they may succumb to alcohol, drugs, or other destructive lifestyle choices!

Don't use this as an excuse to avoid achieving a dream, however.

- Use your fear or stress to propel yourself forwards. Sometimes, the only way to go is up!

- Persistence overshadows even talent as the most valued and effective resource in creating and shaping the quality of life.

> *Genius is 1% inspiration and 99% perspiration.*
> **Thomas Edison**

- If we decide to feel happy now, we will automatically achieve more.

- **Train yourself to feel happy!**

- Be grateful for what you already have. If you feel gratitude, then the Law of Attraction and your RAS will ensure that you get even more to be grateful for!

- Ask yourself:

  o What will this cost?

  o What price will I pay if I don't even try, if I don't move towards this dream?

- It's possible, as you progress towards your dream, that it may no longer seem so important. In this case, create new dreams. Don't use this as an excuse for avoiding a dream that looks hard, however!

WOW Strategy II

Remember *WOW Strategy I* earlier on page 59? I hope you've been depositing your successes on that piece of paper, because it's now time to take it back.

Keep it as a talisman of success. Whenever you need to feel successful, hold it, look at it, and enjoy the feelings you placed there.

Of course, you can always add all your new successes as well!

You can do it!

> Our deepest fear is not that we are inadequate. Our deepest fear is that we are powerful beyond measure. It is our light, not our darkness, that most frightens us. We ask ourselves: "Who am I to be brilliant, gorgeous, talented and fabulous?" Actually, who are you not to be?
>
> You are a child of God. Your playing small doesn't serve the world. There's nothing enlightened about shrinking so that other people won't feel insecure around you.
>
> We are all meant to shine, as children do. We are born to make manifest the glory of God that is within us. It's not just in some of us, it's in everyone.
>
> And as we let our own light shine, we unconsciously give other people permission to do the same. As we are liberated from our own fear, our presence automatically liberates others.
>
> Nelson Mandela,
> quoting Marianne Williamson
> at his Inauguration, 1994

Review

So now we've come to the end of the course and the end of the book.

The process described in this book goes through five major stages. Let's review them together.

The first stage requires us to write down what we want. Although I spoke about goals and dreams, what we were really talking about were desires: hopes, wants and wishes:

Hopes / Wants / Wishes

Figure 17: Overview – Start

Once we start looking at them more precisely, questioning them and ourselves about what exactly they are, how much we want and when we want them, they turn into goals, which are cognitive statements.

Hopes / Wants / Wishes

What?
How much?
When?

Goals   (Cognitive)

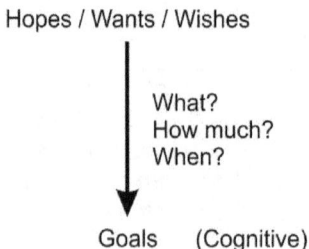

Figure 18: Overview – Wishes to Goals

The questions are best asked in this particular order, because defining what we want, followed by how much of it we want, we are better able to determine how long achieving this goal will take. Of course, not all goals can be pigeonholed this easily, but we do the best we can.

However, goals are little more than desires with deadlines. If they can't be achieved, there's little emotional loss if we downgrade them back to mere wishes. To achieve anything, we must make them much more powerful!

In order to empower our goals, we convert them into well-formed outcomes ("goals on steroids", remember?), using the A-B-C-D-E steps, and then running them through the SMART matrix to check them. Thus, we know not only *what* we want, how much and when, but we also know *how* we'll know when we've succeeded.

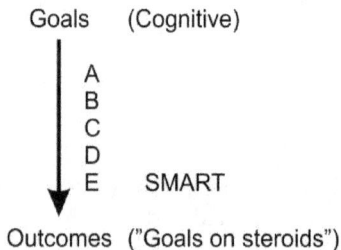

Goals   (Cognitive)

A
B
C
D
E   SMART

Outcomes   ("Goals on steroids")

Figure 19: Overview – Goals to Outcomes

Taking the outcomes, we then add motivation (the "whys") and, especially, emotions, turning them into all-encompassing and all-powerful dreams. These dreams are what give our lives reason, zest and power.

Outcomes ("Goals on steroids")

Add motivation and emotions

Dreams (Affective = emotionally driven)

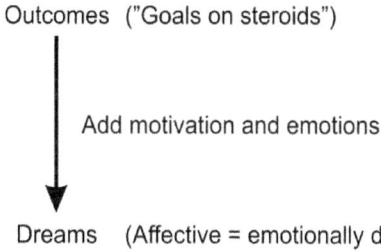

Figure 20: Overview – Outcomes to Dreams

Of course, having created the dream, it's now up to you to actually go out and do something about it! I've given you several tools to help you succeed, but I'm afraid that the rest is up to you!

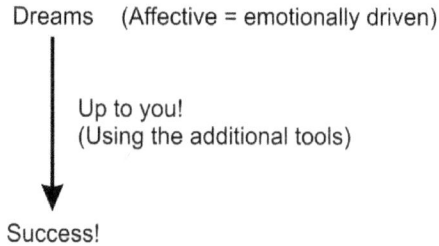

Dreams (Affective = emotionally driven)

Up to you!
(Using the additional tools)

Success!

Figure 21: Dreams to Success

If you follow the five stages, using each of the steps therein, success is something far easier to achieve than many of us could ever have believed is possible.

Hopes / Wants / Wishes

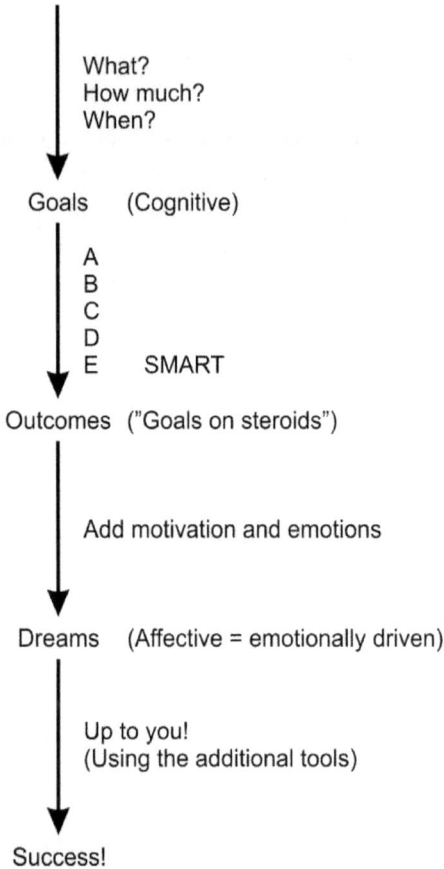

What?
How much?
When?

Goals   (Cognitive)

A
B
C
D
E   SMART

Outcomes ("Goals on steroids")

Add motivation and emotions

Dreams   (Affective = emotionally driven)

Up to you!
(Using the additional tools)

Success!

Figure 22: Overview – All the Steps

Success is the active process of making your dreams real, and inspiring others to dream.
James Anders Honeycutt

Farewell

I hope that the methods and techniques I've taught you here help you achieve the best and most that you can in your life.

> *We need men who can dream of things that never were.*
>
> John F. Kennedy
>
> *Practical people would be more practical if they would take a little more time for dreaming.*
>
> J. P. McEvoy
>
> *If a little dreaming is dangerous, the cure for it is not to dream less but to dream, dream all the time.*
>
> Marcel Proust

I can do no better than leave you with the following advice:

> *Dare to live the life you have dreamed for yourself. Go forward and make your dreams come true.*
>
> Ralph Waldo Emerson

Go and unleash your dreams!

Appendices

Life is just a dream that's come true.
TV advert for *Magner's Cider*

Glossary

Anchor

A particular stimulus that triggers a specific State (q.v.). Examples: the smell of roses reminds you of your first girlfriend, an arm around the shoulder brings back memories of your grandmother, a chuckling baby makes you smile, etc. Anchors can be created consciously or (usually) unconsciously. Conscious anchors can be used to access Resources (q.v.) whenever we want to.

Association / Disassociation

Association: when you see a situation in your mind's eye, you see it through your own eyes.

Disassociation: When you see a situation in your mind's eye, you see yourself as part of the picture.

Break State

Changing the State (q.v.) of your mind and body, by doing something completely different from what you were doing before (stand up, jump around, sing a silly song, whatever you feel like doing).

Ecology

The balance of all parts of a person, body, mind, emotions, beliefs and values, etc. as a whole, as well as the environment around the person (family, friends, work, society, etc.).

Logical Level

The logical levels are a view of the stratification of the human being. It's particularly useful in bringing the various parts of the person into a single alignment. See *Logical Levels* on page 49 and *Alignment of the Logical Levels* on 120.

Meta-Position

A position to the side that, when carrying out an exercise, allows you to "step out of your skin" and look at yourself more objectively.

Modality

Modalities are the primary channels through which a person receives input from the environment, as well as internal communications. NLP recognises the following modalities: sight (visual), hearing (auditory), touch (kinaesthetic), smell (olfactory), and taste (gustatory). Our awareness of reality occurs through these channels. All other inputs (including ESP, intuition, visualisation, etc.) are interpreted in terms of the five main modalities.

NLP

Neuro-Linguistic Programming.

- NLP is a multidimensional model of the structure and function of human experience.

- At one level, NLP charts the dynamic interaction between neural circuitry, physiology, language and behavioural programming, the fundamental components that create subjective experience.

- As a process, NLP is an accelerated learning strategy with a behavioural technology as its by-product. This technology comprises a set of frames, tools and skills for developing systemic awareness, flexibility and competence.

- NLP is also an attitude based on a system of empowering beliefs and presuppositions about the scope of human potential, the process of communication, and change.

Outcome

An outcome is a "super goal", in that it goes beyond a goal: it's a goal with enthusiasm. A goal defines three things: 1) what, 2) when, 3) how much. An outcome also defines how you'll know when you've achieved it. Furthermore, through this definition, it also triggers the RAS.

Resources

States, capabilities, skills, patterns of behaviour, etc. which can be used to achieve an end.

Sensory-Specific

Defines exactly what the senses receive (i.e., what is seen, heard, etc.), without any interpretations. For example, "I see you smiling and laughing" vs. "You look happy". It's exceptionally useful for describing states observed during exercises without value judgements (meanings) being imposed on them.

Stacking

Placing more than one Anchor (q.v.) in a particular place, sensation, etc. This allows us to strengthen the effects of anchors, and also to trigger multiple effects through a single trigger.

State

A particular configuration of the physiology (body), neurology (nervous system) and mind (mental and emotional states). Because the three parts can't be separated, each affects the others.

State can literally change from moment to moment, depending on internal and/or external stimuli. For example, a single sentence can take you from the heights of elation and plunge you into the depths of despair, or vice versa.

It's also used as a neutral description of emotional states.

State, Accessing

Imagining that you're re-experiencing a situation, emotional state, etc. again. See what you saw. Hear what you heard. Feel what you felt. Sink yourself into that experience.

State, Breaking

Terminating a particular State (q.v.). This may be as simple as standing up or opening your eyes, looking out of the window or examining the exact colour of something. Basically, what we're doing is clearing our minds of our previous state and information. *See also Break State previously.*

Submodality

A submodality is a subdivision of the input via a particular Modality (q.v.). It "fine tunes" the information received, allowing a more exact definition of differences.

Bibliography

Books

Bandler, Richard
Using Your Brain For A Change!
Many NLP exercises from one of the founders of NLP.

Bandler, Richard and Grinder, John
Frogs Into Princes
Reframing
Trance-Formations
The Structure of Magic I
The Structure of Magic II
The seminal books which originally defined NLP.

Bliss, Edwin C.
Doing It Now
Setting goals and (mainly) dealing with procrastination.

Getting Things Done
The ABC of time management, alphabetically sorted by subject.

Brennan, J. H.
How to Get Where You Want to Go
Dynamic techniques for achieving success in business.

Burns, David D., MD
Feeling Good
Dealing with everyday problems that get in the way of happiness and success.

The Feeling Good Handbook
A revised version of the above book, with worksheets and many more exercises.

Buzan, Tony
The Mind Map Book: How to Use Radiant Thinking to Maximize Your Brain's Untapped Potential
The best introduction to Mind Maps, their power and how to use them.

Byrne, Rhonda
The Secret
The book that kicked off the present interest in the Law of Attraction.

Collier, Robert
Secret of the Ages
> Although some of the attitudes are dated, the core message shines through as brightly as ever.

Covey, Stephen R.
The Seven Habits of Highly Effective People
> Powerful lessons for personal change. Simple without being simplistic.

Crane, Patricia J.
Ordering from the Cosmic Kitchen: The Essential Guide to Powerful, Nourishing Affirmations
> A quirky, up-beat look at how to manifest what you want in life using affirmations.

Goddard, Neville
Feeling is the Secret
> This is the book that explains what Dr Joe Vitale calls "Nevillizing": using your emotions to empower your goals.

At Your Command!
> A short and simple book about getting what you want.

Helmstetter, Shad
What to Say When You Talk to Your Self
> The title says it all, really.

Kassorla, Dr Irene C.
Go For It!
> How to win at love, work and play.

Kiam, Victor
Going For It!
Keep Going For It!
> Advice and tips on being an entrepreneur, from the man who bought Remington.

Mandino, Og
The Greatest Secret in the World
> 45-week program for personal happiness and success.

McCormick, Elizabeth Wilde
Change for the Better
> Self-help book for creating changes in yourself.

McWilliams, John-Roger and Peter
Life 101
Everything we wish we had learned about life in school – but didn't.

Do It!
Simple, but very powerful, book about goal setting and what prevents us from taking the risks necessary to success.

Millman, Dan
The Way of the Peaceful Warrior
A different look at how to gain what you want, without fighting the world for it.

Pratchett, Terry
The Dark Side of the Sun
A science fiction story in which point of view as a limitation is explored.

Strata
A science fiction story where **we** are the Gods, but have forgotten it.

Robbins, Anthony
Awaken the Giant Within
Giant Steps
Unlimited Power
Three very powerful books on taking control of your life, using NLP techniques.

Rubin, Theodore Isaac, MD
Overcoming Indecisiveness
An eight-stage program for effective decision-making.

Rusk, Tom and Read, Randy
I Want to Change, But I Don't Know How
A step-by-step program for mastering your life.

Schwartz, David J., PhD
The Magic of Thinking BIG
The Magic of Thinking $ucce$$
Maximize Your Mental Power
Three self-help books that touch on goals, achieving them, and how to avoid problems along the way.

Simon, Dr Sidney B.
> *Change Your Life Right Now!*
>> Personal program for changing what you don't like in your life.

Vitale, Dr Joe
> *Life's Missing Instruction Manual*
>> The book you wish you had been given at birth.

> *The Attractor Factor*
>> Great book that teaches you how to get what you want. Now in its second edition.

Vitale, Dr Joe, and Hew Len, Dr Ihaleakala
> *Zero Limits*
>> Getting clear in your life and forgiving yourself.

Wareham, John
> *Staying Ahead*
>> Why we sabotage our efforts, and how we can avoid it.

Wilde, Stuart
> *Affirmations*
>> How to create and use affirmations.

Williams, A. L.
> *All You Can Do Is All You Can Do but all you can do is enough!*
>> How to be a winner in the game of life.

Kindle eBooks

Byrne, Rhonda
The Secret

Burns, David D., MD
Feeling Good

Collier, Robert
Secret of the Ages

Covey, Stephen R.
The Seven Habits of Highly Effective People

Crane, Patricia J.
Ordering from the Cosmic Kitchen: The Essential Guide to Powerful, Nourishing Affirmations

Goddard, Neville
At Your Command!

Helmstetter, Shad
What to Say When You Talk to Your Self

Mandino, Og
The Greatest Secret in the World

McCormick, Elizabeth Wilde
Change for the Better

Millman, Dan
The Way of the Peaceful Warrior

Pratchett, Terry
The Dark Side of the Sun
Strata

Robbins, Anthony
Awaken the Giant Within
Giant Steps
Unlimited Power

Vitale, Dr Joe
Life's Missing Instruction Manual
The Attractor Factor

Vitale, Dr Joe, and Hew Len, Dr Ihaleakala
Zero Limits

Wilde, Stuart
Affirmations

Williams, A. L.
All You Can Do Is All You Can Do but all you can do is enough!

Audiobooks

Collier, Robert
Secret of the Ages

Covey, Stephen R.
The Seven Habits of Highly Effective People

Robbins, Anthony
Awaken the Giant Within
Giant Steps
Unlimited Power

Vitale, Dr Joe
Life's Missing Instruction Manual
The Attractor Factor

Vitale, Dr Joe, and Hew Len, Dr Ihaleakala
Zero Limits

Videos

The Secret

What the Bleep!? – Down the Rabbit Hole Quantum Ultra-Extended Edition

Internet Links

*Dr Joe Vitale (*http://www.mrfire.com/)

*Miracles Coaching Program (*http://www.miraclescoaching.com/)

*The Secret (*http://www.thesecret.tv)

*Write and Publish your own book ... in as little as 7 Days (*http://www.7dayebook.com/)

*My blog (*http://www.stephenoliverblog.com/)

About the Author

Stephen has been interested in personal growth, and the bringing out of the best of people's potential, for well over 40 years. Even as a computer programmer and systems analyst since the beginning of the 80's, his aim has always been to improve the quality of life for himself and others. This interest led him to learn about psychology and growth techniques, resulting in his becoming an NLP Practitioner (Neuro-Linguistic Programming) in 1993.

At the beginning of 1994 he came into contact with Reiki, when he attended a First Degree Reiki seminar run by a Reiki Master of *The Reiki Network*® with his parents. Seeing the improvements that Reiki was bringing to the whole family, they quickly went on to the Second Degree. It became clear to him that Reiki was one of the best tools for the non-invasive support of personal growth that he'd encountered, so he applied for training as a Reiki Master within the Network. He finished his year's training mid-1996, and now gives treatments and teaches Reiki in English and German, in England, Switzerland and Spain.

In 2004 he began a training course as an adult educator, which he completed in the following year. As part of his training, he created the written training concept that The Reiki Network® now uses.

He's presently working on a follow-up book, a fantasy novel, and a series of short story collections.

He blogs at *http://www.stephenoliverblog.com*.

Thank You for Buying This Book

I hope you could help your fellow book enthusiasts out and, when you have a free moment, leave your honest feedback about this book on Amazon. If you don't have the time for that, at least click on the "Like" button. I want to thank you in advance for doing this.

I can be contacted at *admin@stephenoliverblog.com*.

This book is also available as a Kindle version from Amazon. An audiobook version is in the works.